TWAYNE'S WORLD AUTHORS SERIES
A Survey of the World's Literature

PARAGUAY

Luis Davila, Indiana University

EDITOR

Augusto Roa Bastos

TWAS 507

Augusto Roa Bastos

AUGUSTO ROA BASTOS

By DAVID WILLIAM FOSTER

Arizona State University

TWAYNE PUBLISHERS

A DIVISION OF G.K. HALL & CO., BOSTON

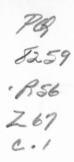

Copyright © 1978 by G. K. Hall & Co.

Published in 1978 by Twayne Publishers,
A Division of G. K. Hall & Co.
All Rights Reserved

Printed on permanent/durable acid-free paper and bound
in the United States of America

First Printing

Library of Congress Cataloging in Publication Data

Foster, David William.
Augusto Roa Bastos.

(Twayne's world authors series ; TWAS 507 ; Paraguay)
Bibliography: p. 125-31
Includes index.
1. Roa Bastos, Augusto Antonio—Criticism and interpretation.
PQ8259.R56Z67   863   78-8061
ISBN 0-8057-6348-1

Para David Raúl, futuro ciudadano
de América Latina

Contents

About the Author

David William Foster, a native of Seattle, studied at the University of Washington, where he received the Ph.D. in Romance languages and literature in 1964. Currently Professor of Spanish at Arizona State University and Chairman of the Editorial Board of the University's Center for Latin American Studies, Professor Foster has taught also at the University of Missouri, Fresno State College, Vanderbilt University, and the University of Washington. During 1967 and 1973 he was a Fulbright Lecturer in Linguistics at various institutes in Argentina, and in 1975 served as an Inter-American Development Bank Professor of Linguistics at the Universidad Católica de Chile.

Professor Foster's research interests include, in addition to contemporary River Plate fiction, medieval Spanish poetry, Spanish bibliography, and Spanish linguistics. He has received support for his research from the United States Office of Education, the Fulbright Program, the National Endowment for the Humanities, the American Philosophical Society, and the American Council of Learned Societies, as well as the research councils of the University of Missouri and Arizona State University. He has published monographs with the University Presses of Washington, Missouri, Kentucky, North Carolina, as well as with Casa Pardo, Scarecrow Press, and Ungar Publishing Company. The University of Missouri Press published his *Currents in the Contemporary Argentine Novel* in 1975. Professor Foster is Associate Editor of *Chasqui* and of *Hispania* and publishes frequent reviews of Latin American literature in *World Literature Today* (formerly *Books Abroad*).

He is the author of *The Marqués de Santillana, The Early Spanish Ballad,* and, with Virginia Ramos Foster, *Luis de Góngora,* all issued by Twayne Publishers.

Preface

Although the critic acknowledges numerous possible approaches to understanding an important novelist, the present study is essentially structuralist in its discussion of the fiction of Augusto Roa Bastos. While attention is paid here to questions of theme and sociopolitical background, references to these topics are meant in the final analysis to be seen in terms of an intrinsic characterization of Roa's novels and short stories. It is for this reason that, in the case of the short stories, only a few titles have been chosen for extensive analysis out of the three dozen that Roa has written. Since Roa has published only two novels, both of them will be examined in as much detail as space permits.

A note concerning the use of the word myth in the final chapter of study: when it is used it should be understood in the sense Roland Barthes, Claude Lévi-Strauss, and other contemporary structuralist critics use it, namely, a narrative formula that is elevated, by the author in the case of literature, to the level of an explanatory representation of human experience and events (see in particular Chapter 5, section IV).

This is the second monographic study on Roa Bastos that I have published, and it is only natural that it bear some resemblance to the first one. However, in *The Myth of Paraguay in the Fiction of Augusto Roa Bastos* only the early stories and the first novel were treated; this study treats also the stories of the 1960s and Roa's most recent novel. None of the material of the first study has been used in the present one without significant alterations, and while the sense of some comments have been repeated here, they are modified by a more detailed emphasis on individual works and by the overriding focus on structuralist issues.

All quotes from Roa Bastos's works are my own unless indicated otherwise.

DAVID WILLIAM FOSTER

Arizona State University

Chronology

1917   Augusto José Antonio Roa born June 13, in Iturbe, in the Guayrá region of Paraguay.

1925?   Sent to Asunción to military school; first contacts with literature in the library of his uncle, the bishop of Asunción.

1934?   Enters military duty for the duration of the Chaco War.

1937   Unpublished novel, "Fulgencio Miranda," wins Ateneo Paraguayo Prize.

1952   Publishes *El ruiseñor de la aurora*.

1942–   Editorial secretary of the Asunción newspaper, *El País*.
1947

1944–   Studies newspaper and radio journalism in England under a
1945   scholarship from the British Council. Has the opportunity to interview De Gaulle after the latter's triumphal entry into Paris. In both England and France, Roa Bastos gives radio presentations on Latin American culture.

1946   Named Paraguayan cultural attaché in Buenos Aires.

1947   February, forced into exile by civil war. Settles in Buenos Aires.

1953   Publishes *El trueno entre las hojas,* a collection of short stories.

1959   *Hijo de hombre* wins first prize in the Concurso Internacional de Novelas de la Editorial Losada in Buenos Aires, which publishes it in 1960.

1960   *El naranjal ardiente*. Writes screenplay for *Hijo de hombre,* recognized as best film in Spanish language of the year. Film receives first prize of the Argentine Instituto de Cinematografía.

1961   Directs the Taller Literario (Writers Workshop) sponsored by Argentine Society of Writers. Travels to Berlin to participate, along with such major figures as Borges, Asturias, and Arciniegas, in a Writers Workshop organized by the German Federation of Writers and the Instituto Iberoamericano de Berlín.

1966	*El baldío*.
1966	Adapts for filming Asturias's major novel on a Latin American dictator, *El señor presidente*. This is one of a number of major Latin American literary works that Roa scripts during this period.
1968–	Prepares screenplay for Leopoldo Torre Nilsson's version of
1969	Güiraldes's *Don Segundo Sombra*.
1970	Returns to Asunción to give courses on Latin American and Paraguayan literature.
1971	Wins a John Simon Guggenheim Foundation Fellowship for creative writers.
1974	*Yo el supremo*.
1976	Accepts an appointment at the Université de Toulouse in France.

CHAPTER 1

The Watcher of the Night: Roa Bastos's Life and Times

I The Archetypic Exile

TO which generation of Latin American literary-artistic exiles does Roa Bastos belong? The question is, of course, more rhetorical than informational. It seems that, almost from the beginnings of cultural activity in Latin America, its writers and artists have repeatedly experienced exile, both self-imposed and imposed by tyrannical regimes. In the sixteenth century the Mexican-born playwright, Juan Ruiz de Alarcón, traveled to Spain in search of a cultural climate that the colonial setting could not afford him. Although he came to be recognized as one of the four greats in Golden Age drama, he was never accepted in Spain because of his Creole birth and his physical deformities, and he remained both a physical and spiritual exile all his life. Later in the same century a young lady, for reasons that are still obscure, "dropped out" of Mexican colonial life, entered the convent and, from within the confines of her self-imposed exile, became Sor Juana Inés de la Cruz, the most brilliant writer in seventeenth-century Latin America.

After independence in the early nineteenth century, exile continued to be a way of life for the Latin American intellectual and writer. The bloody tyranny of Juan Manuel Rosas in Argentina sent major voices like Esteban Echeverría and Domingo Faustino Sarmiento into exile, and José Mármol wrote his only important work, the novel *Amalia*, in exile. Self-imposed exile occurred when men, following the lead of Ruiz de Alarcón, abandoned their homelands in search of greater cultural stimulus than that afforded by a setting that, in terms of the quality of life, did not change significantly with independence from Spain. The Venezuelan Andrés Bello is perhaps

13

the most significant example of this circumstance. For Cuba and Puerto Rico independence did not come, and writers like José Martí, Gertrudis Gómez de Avellaneda, and José María Heredia payed the price of exile for their nationalism.

Perhaps in the late nineteenth century the situation for the artist was a bit better; yet we recall the self-exile from Nicaragua of the century's most important poet, Rubén Darío. After World War I, as economic and political situations worsened, a new generation of exiles emerged: César Vallejo died in Paris, Miguel Ángel Asturias virtually began his literary career in the same city and his recent death occurred in Madrid, and Pablo Neruda moved around Europe and Latin America during several turbulent periods in his native Chile. Buenos Aires, relatively stable during this period, became a haven for the persecuted and the uprooted from all over Latin America and Europe.

In Paraguay the political tone established upon the heels of the independence by that enigmatic Latin American man of the Englightenment, Dr. José Gaspar Rodríguez de Francia, has pre-vailed virtually unmodified to the present day. Paraguay enjoys the dubious distinction of having been the first nation to declare inde-pendence from Spain and the first to have a dictatorial government, the paternalistic tyranny of Francia, The Supreme, based on his highly unique interpretations of the Enlightenment and Rousseau's theories concerning the noble savage. Probably as a result of its unrelieved succession of dictatorships with all of their attendant repression, alleviated only sporadically by futile attempts at demo-cratic government, Paraguay has had very little in the way of a distinguished literary tradition. Yet in recent decades, perhaps stimulated by modern communications, countries like Paraguay have been able to produce major literary voices. But, then, Rubén Darío's emergence from feudal nineteenth-century Nicaragua demonstrates that neither a strong literary tradition nor sustained contact with international culture is an absolute requisite for the appearance of a distinguished literary talent.

Whatever the case may be, Paraguay can boast of a generation—or now in the mid-seventies, of two generations—of very accomplished writers, of which Roa Bastos is undisputedly the titular leader. And both are basically exile generations.[1] In February, 1947, a large segment of Paraguayan intellectuals and political and military leaders attempted a revolution against the dictatorial regime then in power; it was the last attempt at such a revolt and it was a stunning failure. The ensuing chaos sent thousands of Paraguayans into exile, mainly to Argentina, to the frontier areas, and to Buenos Aires. While the Stroessner regime has relaxed its persecution somewhat, many of the writers have chosen not to return, either because repression in their native land continues to be too great for true artistic expression or because, as in the case of Roa Bastos, twenty-five years of exile have left roots that are too deeply embedded outside of Paraguay to permit return. The recent case of Rubén Bareiro Saguier, a poet and Guaraní culture specialist at the Sorbonne who was arrested without explanation while visiting in Asunción, does not augur well for a return of the exiles.[2] So to a great extent Paraguayan culture continues to be a phenomenon in exile. Although it is true that Josefina Pla (she is a Catalan who has lived most of her life in Paraguay, the widow of a major Paraguayan artist) continues to reside in Asunción, hers is essentially the life of a spiritual exile. Even those writers who do live and write in their own country find that their only reliable publishing outlets are in Buenos Aires and elsewhere outside of Paraguay.[3]

II *Paraguayan Roots*

Unlike many Latin American writers who have held important diplomatic posts and, occasionally, the highest office of their land (Rómulo Gallegos was president of Venezuela, although for little more than a year), or who have been involved in sustained and newsworthy struggles for one cause or another, Augusto Roa Bastos has had a relatively uneventful life. Divided between the years of formation in Paraguay (from his birth to 1947) and the years of exile in Buenos Aires (almost an equal period of years), he has led a quiet and unassuming existence, lost in the teeming anonymity of the huge metropolis.[4] Although Roa may regret the long years of separation from his homeland and, more profoundly, from his people, it is significant that he opted to remain in Buenos Aires until his recent move to France. Years of acceptance of an alien way of life have perhaps brought him a privileged perspective toward Paraguay and its problems. And, despite the above-mentioned relaxation of artistic expression in Paraguay, the erstwhile relative freedom of Argentina (at least when compared with Paraguay) is an important condition for a writer who has found his true voice to be the uncompromising exploration of the South American contexts of the human experience, a voice that refuses to align itself with any one political position in order to remain free to express the profound feelings of one of Latin America's most humane men of letters.[5]

Born Augusto José Antonio Roa Bastos on June 13, 1917, in Iturbe, a small village in the Guairá region, Roa grew up in the uneventful obscurity of provincial life. Like virtually all Paraguayans, and especially those of humble origins, he learned to speak both Guaraní and Spanish from birth. Paraguay remains to this day perhaps the most perfectly bilingual nation in Latin America, and the interplay between the two languages is a fascinatingly complex sociolinguistic phenomenon. The result for most Paraguayans is a putatively greater range of verbal expression, shaded by the separate and overlapping uses of the two languages.

For a writer like Roa the bilingual phenomenon has unquestionably represented enhanced linguistic resources for literary creation. On the other hand, there exists a virtually unresolvable tension between a language with an international projection and a language with an identification so bound up with the roots of his people that it is virtually synonymous with Paraguayan nationality.

Roa has discussed the problem that this bilingualism presents to the writer:

[Another] major problem produces structural and procedural problems that are practically insoluable within the context of what might be called—and not metaphorically—a "linguistic pathology." The linguistic polarity—Spanish/Guaraní—turns out to be not an integration, but rather an almost schizophrenic split not only on communicational levels of the spoken language, but also and quite particularly in the literary language. It is a unique and exceptional situation within the cultural and linguistic panorama of Latin America. Throughout Paraguay two languages have cohabitated, eroding each other reciprocally, for four centuries. Spanish is the cultured, "official" language, while Guaraní is the national and popular language *par excellence*. In which of the two languages to write? Guaraní is a spoken language, and its tradition is strictly oral. There exists no [written] literature, and we lack a grammatical systematization of the language and even a uniform orthography to organize syntactic and phonetic values. . . . Why then should one write in Guaraní?

After arguing for the need for the Paraguayan writer to use Spanish as his literary medium, Roa goes on to discuss the unconscious contacts between the popular language and the written language:

Having solved the (procedural) problem of writing in Spanish one is immediately faced with another: where to draw the limits in distancing yourself from your own expressive world [that is, that of Guaraní] so that your "betrayal" is not complete. In other words, how to choose an intermediary point, a semantic combination, that will permit the major part of this country, of this Spanish-Guaraní linguistic area, to understand your texts, to perceive at least their temperature, their natural flavor, if this is possible. And it is, barely.[6]

Suffice it to say that the rural bilingualism to which Roa was exposed as a child has given him one of his most distinctive traits as a writer. His early contact with the *carpincho* hunters, whom he evokes in the first story of *El trueno entre las hojas (Thunder Among the Leaves)*, "Los carpincheros," and with the men in the sugar plant where his father worked is unquestionably an important detail in understanding how his identification with the humble people of his country and with its outcasts stems from his own personal familiarity with them.

Many of the routine details of Roa's youth parallel those of Miguel Vera as told in *Hijo de hombre (Son of Man)*. Like Vera, Roa leads a barefoot existence until shod and sent away by train to military school in the capital at the age of eight. Less than ten years later, although legally underage, he is fighting in the Chaco War against Bolivia. After the war Roa works in a bank and then enters journalism, the testing ground—and the means of economic support—for countless Latin America writers. In the early 1940s he travels extensively among the *yerbales*, the *mate* tea plantations of northern Paraguay. Gathering material for articles in the Asunción newspaper *El País*, Roa familiarizes himself with the life of exploitation and degradation of the *yerbales* workers. Their life has often been considered a national scandal (the Spanish-Paraguayan Rafael Barrett wrote eloquently about the misery of the *yerbales* at the turn of the century), and Roa is to evoke it as one of the narrative motifs in *Son of Man*, his novel on "man crucified by his fellow man."

Roa remains associated with *El País* as both journalist and as editorial secretary throughout the forties until his forced exile in 1947. The highpoint of Roa's journalistic activities comes as the result of a radio program in 1944 and 1945 in which he presented an introduction to English-language literature to a Spanish-speaking audience. The British Council awards him a fellowship for nine months of study in England in 1944 and 1945. He travels throughout that war-torn country and gives radio programs on Latin American subjects for the Servicio de América Latina of the BBC in London. In 1945, the French ministry of information invites Roa to travel to France and Africa, and while in France he is again invited to give radio programs on Latin America. The importance of Roa's European contact should not be overlooked. In the first place Roa's opportunity is indeed unique, for few Paraguayans who are not of independent means are able to travel to Europe and to come into such intimate contact with European journalism and letters. Moreover, Roa is in Europe at a crucial moment. He sees firsthand the devastation of war among nations that had traditionally considered themselves superior to uncivilized Paraguay, and he witnesses the end of the conflict and the flurry of sociocultural assessment that it brought.

During these early years of journalistic activity, Roa begins his literary career in the time-honored Latin American fashion: by writing and publishing poetry in literary supplements (the first apparently dates from 1936). Roa's early poetry is frankly rather bad. He had first come into contact with Spanish-language literature as a child in the ample but traditional library of his maternal uncle, then bishop of Asunción. The bishop's library contained mostly literature of Spain's Golden Age (the sixteenth and seventeenth centuries), and Renaissance and baroque forms of poetic expression are unmistakably present in Roa's early poetry. His first book is published in 1942, *El ruiseñor de la aurora (The Nightingale of Dawn)*, and it is significant that Roa has literally denied its existence by excluding any reference to it in a recent "complete" bibliography of his works.[7] Roa continues to write and publish poetry throughout the 1940s and is also the author of a number of dramatic works that are successfully presented in Asunción. He also writes the novel "Fulgencio Miranda," which is entered in the 1941 contest of the Ateneo Paraguayo; the novel has never been published.

Roa's literary production up until the time of his exile in 1947 is unquestionably apprenticeship writing. This is neither surprising nor unusual. In the first place, Roa did not have behind him the sort of sustained contact with literary creativity that leads to early mature productivity. The image of the young man reading centuries-old poetry in his uncle's library and then imitating it in his own youthful compositions would be charming if it were not basically a pathetic commentary on the plight of the formative writer in some quarters of the world. What is more, in Spain young poets with cosmopolitan contacts were reading the same Golden Age poets that Roa was reading in Asunción and were creating the innovative developments of the Generation of 1927 while the Paraguayan was taking his influence as models to be imitated rather than sources of inspiration to be assimilated. And the lack of any significant developments in fiction or theater in Paraguay during the 1930s and 1940s is one obvious factor in Roa's desire to keep his writing from that period buried. A critic who had at his disposal those writings could undoubtedly show the early manifestations of what are today Roa's greatest strengths and his unquestioned originality in the narrative. Since the poetry is barely accessible and the fiction and theater virtually lost, the best that can be done is to acknowledge the long apprenticeship that the writer had and recognize the limitations of his environment and the time-consuming activities of his journalistic obligations.

III   *Argentine Exile*

In February, 1947, a bloody civil war erupted in Paraguay, and thousands of citizens were killed, imprisoned, or executed; thousands more fled the country. It has been estimated that half a million Paraguayans live in Argentina along the border with Paraguay and in Buenos Aires and other urban centers, constituting an archipelagolike province within the Argentine nation. Gabriel Casaccia has written of the frustrations and sufferings of the Paraguayans who inhabit the frontier zones, the outline of their country physically at hand, but the illusion of ever returning to it receding in their mind's eye. José Luis Appleyard in his 1965 novel, *Imágenes sin tierra (Images Without Land)*, writes of several prototypic—almost archetypic—Paraguayans who inhabit the Buenos Aires metropolitan area, their lives colored by the subconscious image of a distant country that has virtually ceased to be their own (significantly, neither Argentina nor Paraguay is identified specifically in the novel).

Roa leads in Argentina the sort of life in exile that thousands of others have lived. Because of his literary and journalistic talents, he is able to put down roots a bit more firmly than many others have. But there is little question that, like most Paraguayans in exile, he has only with difficulty accepted his life in the Argentine capital. On the level of his unconscious he returns to the experiences of his native past. Because he is a writer, he is able to bring these experiences and the tensions created by their presence in the unconscious onto the level of his creative awareness and to use them as the basis for his narratives. A psychoanalytic critic would undoubtedly make much of the fact that Roa has only been able to produce literature of a universal and international stature as an exile from one culture trapped within another almost totally alien one, sandwiching his writing in between the demanding but economically necessary activities of journalism, book reviewing, teaching, lecturing, and screenwriting. Roa has expressed his own thoughts on the subject:

> [In order to describe my dissatisfaction with my work] we would have to begin with the problems that I had to face when I had choices to make. Hence the defects or the virtues (if such there are) have some possibility of being examined critically in the text that I now reject [*Son of Man*]. For example, the context in which I wrote my first works of fiction: the circumstances of an exiled writer. We might propose an initial approximation to this problem: the sense of a double alienation. On the one hand, the fact that I felt myself to be split off from a very concrete reality, that of my own country. A reality that in turn is segregated from Latin American reality because it consists of a sort of "island surrounded by land," a hole, a void. In any case, an asynchronic reality within the general dimensions of America and its specifically cultural ones. On the one side, this feeling of separation. On the other, the sense of guilt for having accepted this split. Thus the initial supposition of this fiction, the releasing factor, would be the eclosion—the objectification—of a bad conscience. This as concerns the personal circumstance, spiritually, physically, morally, aesthetically, of a fiction writer called A. R. B.[8]

But aside from whether one should interpret Roa's present creativity in psychoanalytic terms as the response to the difficult circumstances of his exile, or whether his residence in Argentina has simply meant the sort of contact with literati and publishers that has brought out the full maturity of his writing, there can be no question that Argentina has provided the context for his finest accomplishments. From the early stories (*Thunder Among the Leaves*, 1953), through his internationally acclaimed prize-winning novel *Son of Man* (published in 1960 by Editorial Losada, which awarded the novel its 1959 Primer Premio, Concurso Internacional de Novelas), to his recent collections of stories and the novel *Yo el Supremo (I, the Supreme)*, Roa has maintained a modest but unerringly superb level of productivity in Argentina. It may be the recognition of this fact, perhaps only subconsciously, that caused him to choose to remain in his adopted country for almost thirty years, the quintessential figure of the writer in exile and—although he would deplore being so called—a symbol of the tragedy of his homeland.

What Roa has written about younger Paraguayan writers may also serve as a form of self-evaluation:

Despite everything, the new promotions of writers and poets find themselves dedicated to the task of furthering this literature in the face of all of the risks and difficulties. They are aware of finding themselves at a farthermost point in historical development, which makes them unusually conscious of the problems of their society. Their fragmented and underground efforts suffer from the defects that stem from this abnormal situation. Nevertheless they do not shrink from it but work with an energy that expresses itself in a language with the force of facts, of the word as act. For them as for those who attempted to change in sign and content the tradition of preindependence Latin American literature, a century and a half after those precursors literary activity has come to signify the necessity for facing up to a destiny, the will to enlist in the vital reality of a collectivity, in its true moral context and social structure, in the complex relationships of a contemporary reality—that is to say, by projecting themselves toward a universal world of man.

Like in René Char's frightening sentence: they do not resign themselves to looking at the night being beaten to death and to remaining satisfied with it.[9]

IV   *A Historico-Cultural Excursus*

When Roa Bastos was growing up in Asunción in the years following World War I, it is difficult to believe that the South American capital had changed very much insofar as culture and intellectual life were concerned in the hundred years since its independence from Spain.[10] Essentially Paraguay was consciously and unconsciously continuing to live an isolation that had become a hallmark of its national psychology. This isolation was not simply geographic. Indeed, during the days of the viceroyalty, Asunción, far up the river from the Atlantic ocean, had been more of a colonial center than Buenos Aires or Montevideo (the coastal areas presented more of a danger to settlers from nomadic Indians than did the heartlands of the continent, where the settled tribes yielded quickly to Spanish domination).

Nevertheless, even during colonial times Paraguay underwent psychological or spiritual isolation. The Jesuits charged with Christianizing the Indians availed themselves of the order's freedom from Spanish political control (the Jesuits owed immediate allegiance to the pope) and imposed a theocratic colonial administration on the lands and natives under their domain. Their goal was to Christianize the Indians by using the latter's own native language, Guaraní, and indeed the Jesuits in Paraguay promoted the Mass and the reading of the Bible in the vernacular at a time when the Counter-Reformation church in Europe was reaffirming the primacy of Latin. An intergral part of the fathers' religious role was the preservation of the Indians from contact with the outside world, especially from avaricious conquerors and, later, rough-and-ready settlers. Conscious in good baroque and Counter-Reformation style of the corrupting nature of the material world, the Jesuits in Paraguay were determined to maintain as isolated and as "Edenically pure" a setting for the Indians as possible. To an extent they were successful: to this day Guaraní is more accepted as a daily means of communication in Paraguay than Spanish, a position of prestige for an indigenous language unparalled anywhere else in Latin America.

The spiritual isolation imposed by the Jesuits left lasting marks on the country. Although the Jesuits were expelled in the latter part of the eighteenth century when they were expelled from Spain (the government at that time resented the Jesuits' political independence, despite the order having been founded by the Spaniard, Ignacio de Loyola), Paraguay was only briefly to enjoy the opportunity to attain the same level of contact with the outside world enjoyed by the other Spanish colonies in Latin America. Paraguay was the first colonial area to declare its independence from Spain (1811). The period that followed independence was marked by turmoil, lack of direction, and competing interests for positions of power. Paralleling Buenos Aires of the same period, some sort of order was not established out of chaos until the emergence of a strong leader, Dr. José Gaspar Rodríguez de Francia (1766–1840). Like Juan Manuel Rosas in Buenos Aires, Francia believed in the virtue of a strong ruling figure and had little use for the ideals of the French Revolution that had sparked revolt and independence movements in the Spanish colonies with such overwhelming success (in Latin America only Cuba and Puerto Rico were unable to free themselves from the rule of the motherland). But where Rosas was simply interested in reasserting a reactionary administrative rule—a few wealthy Creole families were to be in charge in the place of the viceregal government—Francia's goal was to impose an absolute dictatorship based on his personal understanding of the French Enlightenment and his peculiar interpretation of what would be good for the masses.

Francia's rule, which lasted from 1814 to 1840, must be counted as one of the most fascinating phenomena of Latin American history, perhaps unrivaled for the curiosity that it has evoked until Perón's rise to power in the 1940s in Argentina.[11] Francia's goal was remarkably like that of the Jesuits: to preserve the purity of the Paraguayan people and their traditional customs. Unlike the liberals who gained control in parts of South America in the mid-nineteenth century (notably in Argentina when Rosas was defeated in 1852), Francia saw no virtue in converting Latin America into the image of a Europe he saw as corrupt and evil through a lens of almost Old Testament proportions.

Rather, taking his note from Rousseau's quaint notion of the noble savage, Francia aspired to impose upon the Paraguayan people an enlightened dictatorship that would protect them from foreign influences and insure the preservation of their native culture. For almost thirty years he was successful in closing Paraguay off from the outside world, permitting neither entry nor exit from the country and persecuting mercilessly those within the country who disagreed with his policy. Unlike other areas of Latin America, the wealthy and landed Creole families in Paraguay did not assume the reins of political and economic control abandoned by the colonial administration following independence. In fact, Francia had what amounted to a vendetta against the landed oligarchy, for he saw in it a challenge to his ideals. While many of the landed wealthy in Latin America were content to see Latin America continue virtually unaltered after the expulsion of colonial rule (to repeat: rule simply passed from the crown's representatives to the Creoles, with socioeconomic structures and traditional values remaining intact), other elements, often the ambitious nonwealthy, were anxious to establish economic and political reforms that would bring to a feudal society the benefits of capitalism. In Paraguay Francia's challenge came perhaps more often from those Creoles who wanted political control over their own destiny rather than from those who subscribed to the goals of the Argentine liberals.

In either case, Francia was intransigent: power was to remain in his hands in order that he might realize his almost mystical plan for the fulfillment of the Paraguayan people:

These twenty-six years of isolation, of terror, and of astrocious obscurantism were fatal for the culture of the newly founded republic. At the death of the despot, Paraguay found herself in a disastrous spiritual state. "There were no educational institutions, no moral and religious instruction," President López [Francia's successor], declared in 1854 before the congress. "There were a few private primary schools, very poorly off, and time had reduced the clergy to a very diminished number of priests. As far as material matters are concerned, the capital and the towns both offer a most disagreeable picture: propped-up churches that are threatening to collapse, unkempt barracks that are uncomfortable and unsanitary, private homes surrounded by rubble or on the verge of ruin. . . ."

The terror had paralized the spirit of an entire people. The Swiss Rengger, who lived in Paraguay from 1819 to 1827, states that under Francia "even the guitar fell silent, that inseparable companion of the Paraguayan." Hence there was no "literature of the independence" and in the Tibetan isolation imposed by the Supreme One there was not even an echo, until way after 1840, of that movement which was filling the world and was called romanticism. The founding families ruined, the forefathers shot, the jails filled with prisoners, the churches and schools falling down, intellectual life was impossible. . . .[12]

While Francia's regime has usually been described as one of terror, it has suffered from the inevitable distortions of the historians and writers who have dealt with it. Of course it is difficult to speak in favor of Francia's ideals, particularly when one concludes that the present government of Paraguay under Alfredo Stroessner implicitly holds many of Francia's own opinions concerning the virtues of isolation from the outside world and the need to preserve received values and ways of life, particularly the paternalistic "invigilation" of the Paraguayan masses for their own good. Yet it is difficult to believe that the quality of life under Francia was all that much worse than life under Rosas, under Porfirio Díaz, and under a hoard of other dictators, protectors, presidents, so-called enlightened or otherwise. Even in Argentina, which has usually served as the positive model for the development of a liberal society in nineteenth-century Latin America, it is doubtful that the quality of life was decent for any but the (admittedly somewhat numerous) minority in control of the country's destiny, and then only in the littoral and a few other large cities. For the urban masses and for the vast majority of noncity dwellers, even in Argentina life was mostly a problem of subsistence. Revisionist historians have reappraised Rosas's role in Argentine history, and a certain amount of revisionism is in order for Francia. Indeed, it is not impossible to see in his conception of destiny of the Paraguayan people the seeds of what today is called the third-world position, frankly and romantically regionalistic and defiantly anti-developmental and antiprogress.

An excursus on certain historical matters pertaining to Paraguay is important for two reasons. First, it is a conjunction of phenomena to which have been attributed some of Paraguay's unique cultural assets: the preservation and the prestige of the Guaraní language, the dominance of indigenous ways of life (of course, many have been greatly altered over the centuries), the reactionary political values of successive governments that exalt concepts first articulated by Francia, the contradictions of Paraguayan writers and intellectuals who have identified more consistently with the people of their land than any of their counterparts in the rest of Latin America and yet who feel very strongly the need to identify with continental and international cultural values.

Second, the roots of the Paraguayan nation that go back to the Jesuits and to Dr. Francia have played an increasingly important role in Roa Bastos's writings. Where other Paraguayan writers may, like Gabriel Casaccia, focus on the problems of Paraguay from the perspective of international liberal values, Roa Bastos has shown a consistent interest in the nature of the Paraguayan masses and in the impact upon them of the historical and sociocultural roots of his nation. This interest has culminated in his latest work of fiction, the novel *I, the Supreme,* which is Francia's "unconscious autobiography."

CHAPTER 2

El trueno entre las hojas:
The Early Stories

I *Introduction*

IT is not infrequent that, although they may possess excellent qualities when viewed in isolation, the early literary efforts of a writer suffer to some degree from a comparison with what comes to be recognized as his "mature" production. Such is the case with the seventeen stories in Roa's first collection, *El trueno entre las hojas* (*Thunder Among the Leaves*, 1953).[1] It is easy to assert that these stories, with their emphasis on violence, on social injustice, and on the particular circumstances of the Paraguayan experience, anticipate the themes, language, and techniques of Roa's first published novel, *Son of Man* (discussed in Chapter 3). Seen in this fashion, the stories are noteworthy as foreshadowings of the novel and are examined accordingly.

On the other hand, when examined in isolation many of them appear simply to be overwritten. Perhaps this circumstance is due to Roa's turning to fiction after a literary apprenticeship writing highly lyrical and rhetorical poetry. Or perhaps it results from his only partial assimilation of fictional currents of the early 1950s. One can say that Roa is aware of the new "magical realism" in fiction and of the creative potential of combining this mythic conception of human events and nature with socially committed positions.[2] But yet Roa has not been successful in freeing himself from the sort of highly foregrounded regionalism that characterizes the weaker examples of Latin American fiction of the first half of this century.

Roa's unmistakable goal in *Thunder* is to provide a series of stories that represent a characterization of aspects of the Paraguayan experience.[3] Toward this end he chooses topics that constitute focal points

26

of his understanding of that experience. Yet Roa has also become aware of the emerging feeling among Latin American artists that documentary fiction, whether in the form of socialist realism or in the form of regionalism, is simply not an eloquent enough vehicle to represent the complex issues of the Latin American experience. Hence the interest in myth, in magical realism, in variants of European expressionism and, more recently, in structural and semiological experimentation. There is little doubt that Roa avails himself of the general principles of nonregionalist fiction. We realize this in his choice of a highly poetic language, the mixing of Spanish and Guaraní, the use of exceptional circumstances that imply a meaning far beyond the surface texture of sequential events, and the creation of individuals that are less typical in a folkloristic sense and more figurative in a mythic one.

Although many of the stories of *Thunder* have become standard anthology pieces—"La excavación" ("The Excavation"), "El prisionero" ("The Prisoner"), "La tumba viva" ("The Living Tomb")—the seventeen titles are on the whole overwritten, as though Roa had yet to find his own proper level of writing. Certainly it is not necessary to judge a writer's production in terms of a developmental trajectory: often the success of later works highlights the imperfections of early pieces, and it may be difficult to evaluate the latter on their own terms.

In the first extensive review of *Thunder*, Rodríguez Alcalá describes with great accuracy the essential characteristics of these stories:

> One could say, then, that *Thunder Among the Leaves* possesses a profound symbolic meaning. . . . The book is a bitter vision of Paraguayan *humanity*, conceived of as pure nature. It is a sort of epic on the animallike instincts and passions of man that have not yet been transfigured by the dignifying breath of life.
>
> On the other hand, the reader who seeks in this book a collection of Paraguayan landscapes—a torrid and fecund land, with green fields, tropical jungles, broad rivers, and eternally blue skies—will experience total disillusionment. There are no landscapes in *Thunder Among the Leaves*. The book is not an aesthetic vision of the land, but rather an angry protest that expresses itself in the resentful, impotent and irremedial suffering of fictional beings who are flogged by a tragic destiny.[4]

The discussion which follows is based on three of the stories included in *Thunder*. Although no claim is made that these are the best, they are representative of Roa's early quest for adequate fictional structures and of the basic thematic constants of his work.

II *"Los carpincheros": the Context*

"Los carpincheros" ("The Carpincho Hunters") is the lead story of *Thunder;* as such it sets the tone of the entire collection. In it Roa presents a number of basic themes of his work: the elusive mysterious quality of the life of the Indian, whose silence is a mask for violent and unexpected emotions; the contrast between the Indian, locked in the marginal existence imposed by the white power structure, and the foreigner, who exploits the land without understanding its people and their ways; the lack of concern for the indigenous population on the part of the majority of the Europeans (here represented by a group of German immigrants, twice-removed from a sense of the land) and the realization on the part of a few that there is an alternate human experience lived by the natives; the jealously guarded values of "civilization" held by the Europeans and those of tribes like the *carpincheros* who, despite their existence as pariahs of the dominant European society, manage to maintain an ancestral existence with their own forms of freedom and fulfillment.

The story is based on a single event, toward which the narrative builds inexorably. This event is one of unexplained mystery, of—at least from the "enlightened" perspective of European civilization— the horrible intrusion of the unknown into the well-ordered existence of good, solid, hard-working citizens. It is an event that evokes the existence of powerful and extrahuman forces that alter, for one brief moment, the normal routine of life. In one sense we might say that it is an event that, by altering customary patterns of civilized life and by forcing a confrontation between the so-called primitive and the civilized, sets the entire tone of the collection: the overall motif of these stories is the perception of the horrible and the confrontation with the nature of human experience such as to produce in the reader a jolting comprehension of the plight of the society on which the stories focus.

The *carpincheros*—hunters of the South-American rodent, the *carpincho* or *capybara*—are a fierce, nomadic people who inhabit the area of the rivers. Roa refers to them as the only people who have not succumbed to the foreign exploitation described by the story. In his story Roa undertakes to describe a confrontation, a collision between the primitivism of these people and the encroaching civilization represented by the opening up of new lands to immigrant home-steaders. In this case, the homesteaders are a German family—a man, his wife, and their young daughter, Gretchen. They live on the bank of the river where the silent *carpincheros* pass by in their canoes. Roa provides ample pictorial detail of individuals and events, a characteristic of the stories in *Thunder*. One could well insist that the author even dilutes his stories by an overabundance of "poetic" description that diverts the reader's attention away from the underlying human tensions being portrayed.

For example, we might cite the case of the story's basic perspective: Gretchen's interest in and fascination with the primitive *carpincheros*. The young girl, of course, barely speaks any Spanish, much less the indigenous language of the natives. Thus although she is the focal point of the story, she is unquestionably the outsider contemplating a reality from the immense distance imposed by an entire range of cultural differences. Gretchen, in turn, becomes the central actor in the event narrated. Unlike her parents, for whom the natives are presumably simply part of the unpleasant tropical setting to which they must become accustomed if they are to survive, Gretchen takes special note of the natives who travel the waters of the river in their canoes. She is intrigued by them and, ultimately, obsessed with their mysterious nature. Finally, in the fulfillment of the event toward which the story builds, she throws herself into the river after them; she is hauled aboard one of the canoes and carried off into the jungle. Gretchen first becomes aware of the *carpincheros* on the Noche de San Juan, or midsummer's night (which, of course, falls at the beginning of winter in the Southern hemisphere). On this night the inhabitants of San Juan de Borja send burning rafts down the river in honor of their patron saint, St. John the Baptist. With the rafts come the canoes of the *carpincheros*. It is at this point that we can appreciate Roa's attempt to evoke with a highly poetic language a single image that can serve as the central narrative point of reference:

They move along silently. They seemed mute, as though speech scarcely formed a part of their wandering and untamed life. At one point they lifted their heads, perhaps struck also by the three wheat figures watching them pass by from the top of the swirling gorge. A dog or two barked. A guttural word or two passed from one canoe to another, like a piece of tongue tied to a secret sound.

The water was in flames. The sand bank was an immense coal burning red hot. The shadows of the Carpincho Hunters slid swiftly over the bank. The last of the Carpincho Hunters quickly vanished around the bend in the river. They had appeared and disappeared like a hallucination. (*T*, 12)

This passage demonstrates Roa's concern with imagistic, often overly poetic language. But it also demonstrates his interest in suggesting the mysterious and secret quality of the indigenous elements that the European innocents contemplate from the safety of their vantage point high above the swirling waters. The prose itself, highly foregrounded ("a piece of tongue tied to a secret sound"), seems meant to evoke the same state of halluncinated perception that is attributed to the three foreign witnesses. In sum, there is an attempt to suggest rather than simply to report the impact created in the observer by the silent representatives of the unknown elements of the land. Admittedly—and this is the case throughout *Thunder*— the result is more one of overwritten prose. Nevertheless, it does indicate Roa's search for an adequate means of representation beyond simple regionalistic descriptions, a representation that also suggests the complex underlying meanings of the events and people involved in the circumstances described.

The story follows through on a series of contrasts suggested by the passage quoted: the untamed primitivism of the river people versus the "solid" habits of the civilized German immigrants. Gretchen is shown as the pivotal point between these two poles: a part of the latter structure of values, but attracted, in ways that she cannot even realize much less understand, to the silent natives. To this scheme— natives–Gretchen–civilized outsider—is added a fourth constituent, a native with whom she changes places in life when she is carried off by the *carpincheros*. When Gretchen is carried off after throwing herself into the waters, one of the Indians is left behind for dead. In an exchange that seems a bit too schematic, he rises from his coma to take the place of the little girl: between the two opposing sets of values—one primitive and free, the other civilized and circumscribed—there has been a trade. But Gretchen is carried away in a state of semiconsciousness, still fascinated by the allure of the Indians, while the *carpinchero* left behind erupts in violent rage against the situation in which he has been abandoned. Thus, rather than simply an even exchange between the two opposing ways of life, Roa suggests the ultimate captivation of the civilized by the primitive and yet the impossibility of the primitive accepting the constraints of European civilization. The collision between these elements comes with the despair of the parents over their daughter's "escape" into the arms of the *carpincheros* and the fury of the native who is left behind, as he attempts to force his way out of the claustrophobic confines of the immigrants' cabin:

> "Margaret . . . , Gretchen . . . !"
> She runs toward the ravine. The string of canoes is turning the bend among the bonfires. The glow of the fire reveals for a moment, before it is lost among the shadows, Margaret's milk-colored hair. She is like a small moon in one of the black canoes. . . .
> The moment comes when the *carpinchero* rises up from his cot, suddenly turned into a gigantic mulatto. [Margaret's mother] sees him laugh and cry, sees him stumble about like a blind man, bumping into the walls. He seeks an exit. He can't find one. Perhaps death still has him cornered. The laughter can be heard. The sound of his bones striking against the wall can be heard. His whining cry can be heard. . . .
> The rhythmic and muted beat of the *porongo* drum fades away little by little, becoming slower and more tenuous. The last beat is heard as barely more than a drop of blood falling on the ground. (*T*, 23–24)

In one closing image there are evoked the four basic elements of earth, fire, water, and air are evoked, as though Roa meant for the Indians to represent not just a mysterious primitive force that prevails over civilization, but rather the very telluric forces of life itself. In the end, then, the little German girl, impelled by unconscious irrational forces, has "accepted" the primitive values of her new homeland: "Immense teeth of land, of fire, of wind gnaw at the thong of water of the *gualambau* [musical instrument] and make it vomit forth its retchings of hot thunder on [Gretchen's mother's] wheat-colored forehead" (*T*, 24).

While undoubtedly overwritten and in parts perhaps a bit too schematic in its juxtaposition of the primitive versus the civilized and overly dramatic in the event described, "Carpincheros" is still an excellent example of the tone that Roa establishes for *Thunder*.

III   *"Audiencia privada": the Sins of the Weak*

A number of the stories in *Thunder* deal with the topic of human will: the will to survive in the face of insurmountable odds, the will to overcome social injustice, the will to sacrifice oneself for the good of his people, the will to find a private meaning for existence. At the same time that Roa deals with these positive values associated with the free will that Catholic theology ascribes to man, the stories also portray manifestations of will that are part of a collective original sin: the will to control the destiny of others, the will to destroy fragile human existence gratuitously, the will for one to prevail at the expense of his brethren. "Audiencia privada" ("Private Audience") exemplifies the stories of human will. It concerns the role that this aspect of human nature plays in the shaping of the destiny of a people and the necessity for the individual to exercise control over his own frail nature. Although the plot is weak and the juxtaposition of opposites somewhat extreme, the story is interesting for Roa's structuring of the encounter between the strong will of the oppressor and the weak will of the visionary reformer, an event with unquestionably ethical and political implications.

The story involves the stark juxtaposition of the solidly entrenched, corrupt, and pompous minister and a young, eager, and dedicated reformer. The former is visited by the enterprising young engineer, who has drawn up plans for a public works project that will benefit thousands of suffering peasants. Of course, it must be carried out with the consent of the powerful minister, for without his approval there is no hope for its success. Roa sets up the opposition between the two men with considerable detail, providing a caricature of the government official and a sympathetic portrait of the engineer. The story is basically schematic and it is clear that the author has made use of hoary rhetoric in order to "guide" our perception of the fundamental conflict involved between the servant of the power structure and the would-be servant of the people. In this case, the story is one of facile position taking.

However, "Private Audience" becomes interesting in the subsequent modification of the portrait of the engineer. The young man is cursed by a major defect of character that detracts from his positive value from the point of view of the reader's sympathy and allows his positive value within the context of the story to be anulled by the negative value of the minister. The man is a kleptomaniac. The minister has on his desk a set for taking Paraguayan tea; the set includes a golf straw (the *bombilla* used to suck the tea from the *mate* gourd). During an interruption when the minister is out of the room, the man puts the straw into his pocket, it is missed, and he is discovered to be the thief. He is arrested and disposed of, along with the project that would have benefited so many of his impoverished countrymen. No one will miss the detail that the engineer is defeated by his uncontrollable desire to appropriate the valuable objects of the privileged power brokers: the gold straw is a pivotal sign in the narrative between the minus value of the minister and the plus value of the engineer. In stealing the straw the latter unconsciously affirms a desire to partake of the luxuries of the oppressors (luxuries that they can afford because of their exploitation of the masses). For this reason, he is destroyed by the powerful minister and eliminated as a positive symbol for the value system represented implicitly by the reader (who cannot accept the engineer's uncontrollable kleptomania for the artifacts of power).

While the story still continues to be exaggerated in its character delineation—the caricature of the minister and the relatively static, cardboardlike nature of the engineer—the exchange process involving the gold straw and the shift in the value to be assigned to the engineer provide some structural interest. The measure of Roa's caricature and his introduction of the pivotal figure of the gold straw can be taken from the following passage:

"Yes, your project interests me. This work will be carried out. We'll do it together, you and me. You as the author of the idea. I as the government's man. Of course, if the government isn't in on it, nothing can be done. We want all works of progress to be governmental, official. It's our constant concern. For the well being, the happiness of the people, we are ready to spend, to sacrifice anything."

The parrot screeched with its strident laughter from his bamboo perch. It sounded like the laughter of a dwarf.

The office-helper reappeared with the tea. The thick lips once again began to suck the straw sonorously. The voice of the minister became amiable, friendly. (*T*, 64)

The general sense of the text is obvious: the engineer fails because he lacks complete control over his person, because he is attracted to the valuable artifacts associated with oppressive power. The constrastive effect is heightened by the engineer's need not to fail in an undertaking that would benefit so many unfortunate peasants. But Roa's judgment is harsh: the young reformer's lack of adequate will and control is an irremediable failing in the world of cruel political realities in which he must operate.

IV   *"La excavación": A Dead-End for Man's Liberation*

One of the key stories in *Thunder* is "La excavación" ("The Excavation"). It belongs to a group of stories that involve individuals who can be called Roa's figures of the true Paraguayan man. Roa is concerned with individuals who run the gamut from unconscious suffering to the intial stirrings of the sort of awareness of self that revolutionary commitment demands. Such a commitment may involve the open assumption by certain individuals of a sacrificial role that they fervently believe will contribute to the liberation of their people. This type of individual is to be found in the title story, "Thunder Among the Leaves," where Solano Rojas is a prefiguration of the Christ figures in Roa's first novel, *Son of Man*. The spirit of sacrificial responsibility of these figures is summed up by Solano in a charge to his fellow Paraguayans, who must be led out of their silent bondage through the sacrifice of men of redemptive commitment: " 'Never forget, my sons, that we must always help each other, that we must always be united. The only brother that a poor man really can count on is another poor man. And together we all form the hand, the humble but powerful fist of the workers . . .' " (*T*, 190; this statment uses both Spanish and Guaraní words). While this sounds like rather standard Marxist revolutionary rhetoric, Roa couches it in the same sort of quasi-mythic context to be found in the opening story of the collection. Rojas's death, which results from his leadership of the workers in a strike against the implacable owners of a sugar refinery, is given not only a "socialist" meaning, but a mythic one as well: "The river was a good tomb, green, circulating, calm. It received its dead sons and bore them without protest in its arms of water that had rocked them at birth. A little later it brought piranhas so that they would not rot in long and useless navigations" (*T*, 208).

In "The Excavation" we have less of a sense of revolutionary commitment on the part of the central figure and more the personal struggle for survival, born of an awareness of circumstances that leads to sacrificial commitments. The story is political in nature and relates the efforts of a group of political prisoners to escape from the cell in which they are being held. They die one by one in the attempt, the tunnel that they are excavating in the struggle to attain physical freedom is discovered, and the few who remain alive are summarily executed for their efforts. The story is metaphoric of man's spiritual imprisonment by social injustice and of his strivings for self-liberation; in the end, the simple fact is that those strivings are frustrated with his annihilation by the forces that oppress him. The metaphoric value of the story is carried through with the symbol of the tunnel—the arduous conduit of the individual's movement toward liberation—and the story is effective in portraying the enormous physical suffering of the prisoners in their incarceration and in the overwhelming obstacles presented by attempts to attain freedom through the laborious excavation of a subterranean tunnel.

The story, then, has several apparent levels of meanings; that is, it can be viewed as a composition that invites parallel readings.[5] The most obvious level is political: the harsh, unrelenting portrayal of tyrannical oppression in all of its boundless cruelty. A secondary level, dependent on the political one, concerns the futility of endeavors at liberation in the face of certain failure and annihilation. The ethical basis of society is neutralized by the existence of forces—entrenched dictatorships, imperialistic exploitation, foreign domination—that thwart natural human aspirations (Roa's work throughout assumes, of course, that man is endowed with a range of natural aspirations that, once made conscious of their lack of fulfillment, he strives to attain). The intensity of the effort expended in the excavation is completely vitiated by the discovery by the authorities of the prisoners' escape attempt.

A third level of the story is more generalized in mythic terms: the prisoners are seen not simply in terms of their futile attempts to free themselves from an unjust imprisonment, but as engaged in liberating themselves from an all-encompassing oppression signified by the choking morass of mud through which they must make their escape. Here man's subconscious is evoked, and the prisoners are endowed with a level of mythic awareness that highlights the importance of their struggle to escape:

> The earth, dense and impenetrable, was now, in the epilogue of the mortal duel begun long ago, what wore him down tirelessly and began to eat him, still alive and warm. . . . He began to remember.
> He remembered that other subterranean mine in the Chaco War, long ago. A time that now seemed to him to be a fantasy. He remembered it, nevertheless, clearly and in all its details. . . .
> The entire highlands, stony, desolate, descended, drawn by the moan of the *cuecas*. An entire race made of copper and punishment descended from their cosmic platform to the voracious dust of the trenches. And from the great river, from the great Paraguayan forests, from the heart of his people, also absurdly and cruelly persecuted the *polcas* and *guaranias* descended too, joining together, becoming brothers to that other melodious breath that

rose up from death. And thus it was because it was necessary for the people of America to continue to die, to continue to kill each other, in order for certain things to be expressed correctly in terms of statistics and the market, of currency exchanges and correct exploitations, with exact figures and numbers, in the bulletins of international plunder. (T, 73; the italicized terms in the passage are South American native dances.)

Continuing the flashback and the confusion of the levels of time and event in the feverish mind of the prisoner on the verge of both escape and suffocation, the story stresses how the individual effort is figurative of the struggle of an entire people:

That tunnel in the Chaco and this tunnel that he had himself suggest they dig in the floor of the jail, that he personally had begun to dig and that, finally, had served him only as a mortal trap—this tunnel and that one were one and the same: a single hole that opened up straight and black and that, despite its straightness, had surrounded him from the time he was born like a subterranean circle, irrevocable and fatal. A tunnel that was now forty years old for him, but that in reality was much older, really immemorial. (T, 75)

In this fashion, the tunnel is transformed into a static symbol. It is a symbol not only for the prisoner, for whom it represents a lifetime of endless, useless struggle against oppression, but it also represents the narrative's emphasis on the unceasing yet seemingly futile collective struggle of an entire people. Life is a black and bottomless pit (or endless tunnel) in which a sector of mankind is permanently trapped. The suffering individual's conscious perceptions—the unconscious witness of a circumstance raised to the level of myth—is the central, controlling force of the story. And when those making the escape attempt are discovered and executed, it is not only a group of unknown unfortunates who are liquidated. It is the annihilation of a group of figures of a suffering collective identity. Despite the tremendous effort expended and, ultimately, wasted by the prisoners, the journalists who are invited to examine the tunnel are indifferent to the desperation it bespeaks, and oblivion reigns as the incident is forgotten in the daily course of events.

V   *Conclusions*

"The Excavation" is a key story in *Thunder* because it joins the theme of the human struggle for liberation with a bleak realization of the little chance of success for that struggle. Unlike the title story

"The Excavation" does not offer the image of facile revolutionary accomplishment, and as a consequence it is more satisfying for its sober judgment that oppression is likely to remain a way of life for the Paraguayan people for the foreseeable future. (This sober judgment also underlies the portrayal of revolutionary figures in Roa's novel *Son of Man.*)

The stories of *Thunder* are variations on themes associated with Roa's perception of the Paraguayan experience, and the three that have been examined in detail in this chapter exemplify cardinal points in that perception. While a good number of the stories are technically and artistically defective because Roa had yet to find a balanced literary voice, they are valuable for the seriousness of the author's attempts to elaborate the themes and symbols with which he chooses to deal.

CHAPTER 3

Hijo de hombre: *The Christ-Symbol Accommodated*

I *Introduction*

WHEN Roa Bastos published *Hijo de hombre* (*Son of Man*, 1960)[1] he had been residing in Buenos Aires for approximately ten years. During that time he made his definitive break with the poetry of his early literary career and, in the process of finding the most appropriate vehicle for the expression of his vision of the Paraguayan experience from the perspective of the exile, turned definitively to prose. Although he permitted the publication in 1960 in a small collection entitled *El naranjal ardiente* (*The Burning Orange Grove*), the poems on the topic of exile written in Buenos Aires have remained essentially unpublished. The stories of *Thunder Among the Leaves* are also evidence of the struggle of the exile to find an adequate voice, yet many of them are flawed by an exaggerated "poeticness" and by errors in handling human motivation.

Son of Man is especially important in Roa's literary biography precisely because it is such an overwhelming success as a novel. Moreover, both its story line and its structure reveal a concern for the ambiguities of the human condition, while at the same time they are the vehicles of what is unquestionably a well-formed vision of the historical experience of the Paraguayan people. It is a vision that stipulates its own historical projection beyond the immediate context of the novel in terms of the salvation of the Paraguayan people to be wrought by the figures that the novel evokes.

Roa has expressed considerable dissatisfaction with this novel and has been reluctant to publish subsequent fiction. It is for this reason that the reader cherishes the handful of short stories that have appeared since *El trueno* and why the 1974 publication of the novel

Yo el Supremo was an important event. Roa's dissatisfaction is a very understandable restlessness on the part of any serious artist with what he has produced: the realization that one can never be satisfied with his work because art will always fall short of the demands placed upon it by the artist and his public. In the case of *Son of Man* Roa's dissatisfaction may extend to certain problems of structure that were not completely resolved, like the alternation of narrative voices discussed in the last section of this chapter, the use of a considerable amount of potentially misleading Christian symbology, and the implication, supported by the fact that the framework of the novel follows a partially historical trajectory, that the liberation of the Paraguayan people from their age-old suffering is more imminent than is realistically possible.

Central to *Son of Man* is the juxtaposition of two figures: Miguel Vera and Cristóbal Jara. Although in the final section of this chapter we take up the problem of narrative voice, with which the juxtaposition of these two figures is bound up, it should be noted that Vera and Jara are touchstones for the narrative. Vera, a son of the Paraguayan petite bourgeoisie, narrates at least half of the novel's nine chapters (the odd-numbered ones). Vera is romantically committed to the need for social revolution in Paraguay, a need that he articulates well enough so that he is, in part, an identifiable persona of the author. Yet, because of his romanticism and other personal failings, he is unable to contribute to that revolution. In fact in the end Vera becomes as much of a force for continued oppression as the official enemies themselves, and in this detail we can see him as a Judas figure. Jara, on the other hand, in unquestionably the "son of Man," the Christ figure, the man who, if not in person, through the force of his character and its effect on those who follow him, will lead his people out of their bondage. Inarticulate, silent, untutored, Jara, the antithesis of Vera, is a Christ figure, not in any paradigmatically Christian sense—Jara fails to bespeak the values of Christianity that the forces of oppression have expropriated for their own nefarious use—but in the degree to which he symbolizes the potential for the salvation of mankind by man himself, by the forces of human social redemption incarnate in a man of the people.[2]

Of course Roa is not original in his use of a Christ figure, and it would be naive to believe that either Roa's identification of Jara as a Christ figure, the Son of Man, or the critic's characterization of the author's carefully developed figure represents any allegiance to traditional Christian or Catholic beliefs. Like innumerable contemporary writers, Roa sees in the Christ figure a powerful symbol of the redemption of man by man himself, a symbol that has been perverted by official religious dogma and its subservience to oppressive political regimes.

II *Narrative Structure*

The direct narrative of *Son of Man*—the surface texture that the reader experiences linearly—covers at least a twenty-year period, from sometime before 1912 to 1936, the period leading up to the Chaco War with Bolivia (1932–1936) and the period immediately following it. Although it is easy to be precise about the termination of the novel since the narrative ends with the description of Miguel Vera's suicide right after the conclusion of the Chaco War, it is more difficult to fix the actual point in time at which the novel begins.

The first chapter recounts Vera's recollections of the town derelict, Macario Francia, and his tales concerning the days of the Francia dictatorship in the mid-nineteenth century. These tales include the life of Gaspar Mora, the leper who carves the famous Christ of Itapé. Rodríguez Alcalá has based himself on this procedure of Vera's recalling Macario, who in turn recalls the earliest days of the Paraguayan nation, to assert that the chronological span of the novel is, in fact, all of Paraguayan history from the now mythic days of the Francia regime up to the time of the harsh present of the Chaco War.[3] Nevertheless, *Son of Man* is in no way a historical novel; nor is it even a mythic novel in the sense that it seeks to present a unified vision of the Paraguayan experience. If it were the latter, we would expect greater superficial correlation with all of the significant events of that nation's history. Yet, the only direct allusion to the Great War of the Triple Alliance (1864–1870), in which the male Paraguayan population was virtually extirpated in armed conflict with Argentina, Brazil, and Uruguay over questions of national boundaries, comes in the second chapter: an enigmatic Russian doctor exiled in Sapukai discovers that the religious idols brought him by his patients in payment for his generous services contain gold and silver hidden away by wealthy families at the time of that conflict.

The Great War is customarily considered a turning point in Paraguayan history, the culmination of Francia's isolationism and almost paranoid concept of the nationalization of the Paraguayan "noble savage." At the same time, the havoc wrought by the Great War and the adjustment of the survivors to it underlay the foundations for much of what Paraguay is today. Yet once we have left behind the first chapter and its partial evocations of the Francia legend via the rambling mind of Macario (and often the legend is evoked strictly in terms of the old man's own life, rather than in terms of consecrated popular beliefs of which he can be called the vox populi bearer), the remaining nine chapters follow rather closely events that take place in the twentieth century pertinent to the biographies of the novel's two antithetical figures: Miguel Vera (his childhood is first brought up in chapter 3, which, chronologically, precedes chapter 2) and Cristóbal Jara (his birth in the *yerba mate* planatations is described in chapter 4). Thus, while there is a vague chronological framework for *Son of Man,* there is only slight justification for seeing it as an attempt to plot the spiritual trajectory of Paraguayan history. Whether or not the novel does in fact, deal with values, both positive and negative, that define the Paraguayan "being" is quite another matter, one more germane to a sociological interpretation of the novel.

The nine chapters that make up *Son of Man* are in many ways autonomous narratives, and one is tempted to say that each could stand on its own as a short story. Of course it is difficult to assert this without implying that the narratives themselves are not interrelated in such a way as to constitute a unified novel. Indeed, it is precisely the degree to which the individual narratives are interrelated that makes it impossible for anyone who has studied the novel at length to see the nine chapters as so many short stories. And yet Roa has taken care to give each chapter a radical degree of internal unity. Moreover, several of the chapters have appeared in collections along with legitimate short stories. Conversely, in our analysis of Roa's short stories from the 1960s we will see that the first five entries in *Moriencia (Slaughter)* are claimed to be segments of an unpublished novel that has yet to be assembled as such. Although we need not belabor the point, it should be apparent that Roa has at least a marginal interest in experimenting with narrative units that can be structurally dependent as well as structurally interdependent units in a larger narrative.

One of the ways in which the nine segments are structurally interrelated is on the basis of narrative voice. Narrative voice is a major problem in the novel, for it is questionable whether all nine chapters are narrated by Miguel Vera or whether he relates only the odd-numbered ones (there is internal evidence that at least the latter is true). If Vera is not the narrator of the even-numbered chapters, it is unclear who is. More on this matter in the last section of this chapter. Whatever the narrative "origin" of the nine chapters, they seem at least to have been brought together by Vera himself (or does he bring together only the odd-numbered chapters written by him, the novel being the result of alternating those chapters with chapters by an unidentified narrator?). The final pages speak of a manuscript found (that is, the novel itself) by someone else, thereby providing "documentary" validation of its existence. To whatever extent the narrative is an indictment of Miguel Vera, the pseudodocumentary framework provides a confirmation of both his character and his oblique witness of the Paraguayan circumstance. Roa presents the narrative as having been transmitted to him by the person who discovered it:

(From a letter from Rosa Monzón)
    " . . . Thus ends Miguel Vera's manuscript, written on the backs of odd sheets of official writing-paper and stuffed into a leather haversack. He finished writing it shortly before the accident in which he was shot in the spine. The ink on the last pages was still fresh; the last paragraph was scrawled in pencil.
    "When I went to Itapé with Doctor Melgarejo to fetch the wounded man, I found the worn haversack. It was hanging at the head of his bed with the manuscript inside it. I took it with me, certain that it contained the key to an understanding of this man who now lay helpless and in pain. There were conflicting versions of how the accident occurred; some said that the gun had gone off while he was cleaning it; others that it had gone off while the child [his companion] was playing with it. The inquest decided in favour of the former version . . . [my ellipsis].
    "Some years have passed since these events, and now when the country is once again on the brink of civil war, with the oppressors on one side and the oppressed on the other, I have decided to look out [sic] his papers and send them to you, now that he 'can neither withdraw, nor hesitate, nor yield. . . .' I have copied them without changing a comma. I have only left out the paragraphs which concern me personally; they are of no interest to anyone.
    "It seems to see [sic for me] that the principal value of these stories lies in the testimony they contain. Perhaps their publication will help, in however small a degree, to make people understand the much-slandered Paraguayan race, which for centuries has swung between oppression and rebellion, between the ignominy of its tyrants and the glory of its martyrs. . . ." (H, 254–55; ellipses in text.)[4]

    With the exception of the last paragraph, which may be read as an epilogue to the novel, Monzón's entire statement has strong ironic overtones. In the long paragraph omitted at the end of the second paragraph, Miguel Vera is described by Rosa Monzón as an introvert, a sentimentalist, a bit of an aboulic, a pathetic figure who observed the tragedy of his people from the sidelines. Yet one cannot be certain as to the objectivity of this assessment. The last sentence of the penultimate paragraph indicates that she enjoyed a close relationship with Vera, and it would not be difficult to conclude that her portrait of the man, along with the purportedly unedited manuscript, may have been affected by this relationship. In other words, Monzón's letter of transmittal is not completely disinterested. This may be only a gratuitous complication of the novel, or it may correspond to a deliberate attempt to reduce all statements and interpretations in the novel to a level of conjecture in order to escape the trap of ultimate pronouncements often found in "committed" novels.

In any case, and despite whatever reservations Monzón's letter signals as to Vera's personality, the novel is, at least as concerns the segments directly attributible to Vera, a personal statement by one man who is unquestionably tortured in mind and spirit by the plight of man as he sees it around him. Vera's writings—the whole raison d'être of the jumbled papers is, as Rosa Monzón suggests, the escape toward desperation, toward symbols. Vera strives to organize a representation of the experience of a people and whatever organization he does achieve is imposed on the novel as a whole through a symbolically interpretative fiction. All of the chapters of the novel deal with a specific range of symbols of which the Christ is the most dominant, given form by both individual human experiences and the carved figure left by Gaspar Mora for the people of Itapé. Throughout the novel these figures serve to identify a unified mankind, enslaved by the diabolic forces of the Paraguayan power structure and foreign exploitation; yet it is a mankind that can, through the realization of its own inherent values, bring about its own salvation and redemption from enslavement. Despite reservations concerning a unified narrative structure and questions concerning Vera's personal commitment to profound revolutionary principles, *Son of Man* is unquestionably unified in the presentation of these symbols in a coherent fictional pattern.

Son of Man, while possessing one organic unity of plot, is divided, by vitue of quasi-autonomous narrative units, into four major segments: the stories, respectively, of (1) Gaspar Mora, the leper who, in his self-imposed flight from civilization to protect it from his disease, carves the Christ of Itapé; (2) Alexis Dubrovsky, the exiled Russian doctor who practices for a time in Sapukai; (3) Cristóbal Jara, the prototypic revolutionary figure caught up in the Chaco War and killed attempting to bring water to besieged forces at the front; and (4) the epilogue of the novel in which Miguel Vera, the dominant voice of the novel, commits suicide after describing the pathetic human wrecks of the "heroic" Chaco War. An examination of *Son of Man* from a structural point of view best centers on the intertwined stories of Mora, Dubrovsky, Jara, and Vera. The following outline demonstrates interrelationships that the following sections will detail:

I.   Roa Bastos, author
II. A. Rosa Monzón (reliable?) editor
     B. Miguel Vera (exclusive?) narrator of the stories of 1–3
        1. Gaspar Mora, sculptor of the Christ of Itapé
           a. Macario Francia, his "biographer"
           b. María Rosa, lover (?) of Mora, and guardian of the Christ
        2. Alexis Dubrovsky, Russian doctor
           a. Damiana, Vera's servant, and
           b. People of Sapukai, including the lepers;
           c. María Regalada, gravedigger, and
           d. Alejo, her son by Dubrovsky
        3. Cristóbal Jara, "The Son of Man"
           a. His parents
           b. María Regalada (see 2b)
           c. Juana Rosa, redeemed prostitute
           d. The lepers
           e. The people of Paraguay

III   An Organizing Symbol: the Christ of Itapé

Son of Man turns on two Christ figures. The first is a leper by the name of Gaspar Mora whose story is told in the first chapter. Mora leaves behind at his death a life-size carving of Christ that, despite the horrified protestations of the clergy, becomes a symbol of his fellow citizens of Itapé, a representation of their earthly sufferings as human beings. The second figure is Cristóbal Jara, already mentioned as the antithesis of Miguel Vera, the narrator who tells how he betrayed Jara's band of insurgents. Jara, who dies during the Chaco War carrying water to besieged troops at the front, is presented in chapters 4–6 and 8 as the embodiment of the "son of man," the individual who will take it upon himself to bring about the release from bondage of his fellow men. Unlike the Christian redeemer, Jara is an inarticulate individual who never becomes a great leader of men. Yet in his simple faith in human dignity, in his activities as an insurgent leader, and in his sense of mission in the face of the experience of his people, the rhetoric of the novel makes it abundantly clear that he is the antithesis of both the oppressors of mankind and the "intellectuals" who articulately sympathize with the need for revolution, but who are incapable of action and who thus become the unknowing abettors of oppression.

Of course both Mora and Jara are Christ figures to the extent that suffering of the Christian redeemer has become, apart from its institutionalized interpretation, symbolic of a fundamental human circumstance in the Western tradition: man's sense of spiritual/political enslavement and the inborn need to redeem his dignity through a liberation from that enslavement. Such a liberation must be won through great sacrifice on the part of the individual and almost inevitably through the "passion" of a victim who takes upon himself the burden of all mankind. Often these Christ figures are mockeries of the institutional Christian redeemer, either because Christianity is seen as no longer able to address itself to the problems of human suffering and enslavement or because the church itself has become the servant of the oppressors, thereby vitiating the power of its own canonical Christ figure. Roa's Christ figures are inversions of the traditional figure in both of these senses.[5] Roa nevertheless uses the Christ symbol rather than other possible symbols precisely in order to evoke its "secular," humanistic meaning. At the same time he underlines how that primitive meaning is today more valid than the all-pervasive yet inefficacious meanings of stagnant Christian institutions.

In the first chapter, which gives its title "Son of Man" to the novel as a whole, Roa presents both the legendary background for the novel and the basic figures of Christ made man and man made Christ.[6] The ambivalence over the relationship Christ/man is central to the vision of Paraguayan experience put forth by Roa in his work. Referring to a figure of Christ that now stands as a landmark outside of Itapé, the narrator, Miguel Vera, comments on what it represents for the people of his native village:

[One] relic of former times remains. About a half a league from the village rises the hill of Itapé. The high-road passes the foot of it, crossed by a stream formed by the spring which rises on the hill. At certain hours of the day, when the light is right, it is possible to see, silhouetted against the rosy incandescence of the sky, the shelter which protects the figure of Christ on the top of the hill.

That is where mass used to be celebrated on Good Friday. The people of Itapé had their own liturgy, and the tradition soon became a legend. . . .

It was a harsh, primitive rite, an expression of the villagers' rebellious spirit which, as though roused by the smell of sacrificial blood, broke out on Passion Friday in this demonstration of fear and hope and anger.

This was the ceremony which gave to us villagers of Itapé the name of fanatics and heretics.

It cannot be denied that in these annual rites the villagers seemed to regard the Christ as a victim they wanted to avenge and not as a God who had died willingly for men.

It may have been that the mystery was too deep for their simple minds. Either he was God and therefore could not die. Or he was a man. If he was, his blood had been shed in vain as far as they were concerned. For they had not been redeemed; things had only changed for the worse.

Perhaps it was simply the origins of the hill-top Christ which had wakened in their hearts this strange belief in a redeemer as ragged as themselves who, like them, had been constantly mocked and ridiculed and persecuted, ever since the world began. Such a belief was, in itself, a reversal of normal faith, a permanent incitement to revolt. (*H*, 8–9)

Of primary importance here in understanding how Roa makes use of his eminently Christian symbol is that the Christ honored and venerated by the Itapeños is one which has been born of them and of their suffering; he is also a Christ that testifies to the suffering of a redeemer in order to save them from their terrible plight. Yet what we have is not simply a "folkloric" accommodation of an institutional concept that is too difficult for the people to comprehend correctly. Of course we may speak of a misunderstanding here: the people have taken a canonical figure and given it a new meaning; a meaning conforming to their particularly spiritual preoccupations and attributable to the figure to the extent it is not present in its canonical usage. That is to say, the Christ figure of the church does not address itself to the real suffering of the people and, as the result of a set of fortuitous circumstances, the people have taken that figure and given it an extended—accommodated—meaning that evokes for them the suffering that the church and the government it supports have refused to recognize. This new Christ is a human symbol of a God that, in turn, represents their release from suffering. By the same token, it is a symbol of man who can become God-like in his redemptive role. This "son of man" dies by the hand of man for the sins of man, and it must be a son of man who will free mankind from the cross of its suffering. This Christ may be unquestionably anthropomorphic in its conception, but the son of man who will die for the salvation of these people can only be one of their own. Hence the greater identification of the Itapeños with Gaspar Mora's rough-hewn figure than with the stylized crucifix of the church.

The fortuitous circumstances by which the people of Itapé acquire their own secular Christ figure is recounted by Miguel Vera in the first chapter of the novel. Construed as a series of flashbacks, Vera's story (the most important of a number of incidents that he recalls from his childhood) evokes first the old derelict Macario Francia and, through him, Macario's nephew, Gaspar Mora. Whereas Vera is the voice throughout the novel of an educated Paraguayan minority, a voice often partronizing in its professed sympathy for the suffering of the people, Macario speaks as the collective unconscious of that people. His stories, which Vera ostensibly repeats as he heard them as a child, have all of the earmarks of a legend, of myth, of the unconscious values of a people turned into popular tales. Macario's story of Mora springs from his unconscious depths and is presented as the ramblings of a senile old man. Yet for Vera and for the reader, it articulates fundamental popular belief and values.

A maker of musical instruments, Mora contracts leprosy, a common affliction in tropical Paraguay. He takes refuge in the woods, lives in isolation, and at one point carves himself a figure of Christ. When Macario is found dead, the figure is found with him. Each one of these aspects of Mora's sickness and death holds for Macario—and, therefore, for the people for whom he is the guardian of the legend—a larger meaning that has increased with the passage of time and with the fame of the figure set on the hill outside of Itapé. For Macario, the mythic teller of the people, Mora was, in his own way, equally a voice of the people, who used his musical instruments, especially his guitar, to give expression to the deep pathos of their lives:

I can remember how, as darkness was falling, Gaspar would begin to strum the guitar he was making, to test the tone of the instrument. People would lie down on the grass to listen. They would come out of their huts. Even the hill seemed to be listening, and the river. The distant music of the guitar always brought tears to my mother's eyes. My father would usually just have come back from the cane-fields and he would try not to make a noise with his tools.

Even after Gaspar died in the *monte,* we would sometimes hear the guitar. As Macario's shaky voice died away in the hush of the falling darkness, while the blue sparks of the fireflies were being kindled all around us, we would hear very faintly, as though from under the earth, or from the depths of our memories, the sound of Gaspar's music. (*H*, 17)

Gaspar Mora as myth is not only a figment of Macario's senility, but a vital reality to the people as well. They listen to his guitar with tears in their eyes, as if hearing the distillation of their eternal suffering in his music. Moreover, Mora is presented as almost priestly in person and morals (Macario insists, erroneously according to Vera, that Mora died a virgin), and the leprosy he contracts is symbolic of the suffering that he assumes in the name of the people. Leprosy is still a common occurence in tropical Paraguay. But throughout the novel it is made to identify the social outcast, an objective manifestation of the circumstance the mass of the Paraguayan people are forced to live in. Ths Russian doctor Dubrovsky devotes much of his energies to caring for the lepers and constructs a sort of colony for them on the outskirts of Sapukai. Later, while fleeing from government agents who are pursuing him for his revolutionary activities, Cristóbal Jara makes his escape with the assistance of the lepers. In the case of Mora, the disease is a dramatically physical manifestation of the very human suffering he evokes in his music. Thus there is little question that in *Son of Man* leprosy is one of the major correlatives of a particular human condition.

Mora's disease obliges him to flee the village, both because he wants to protect his fellowmen from infection and because he prefers to suffer in ascetic solitude the leper's slow death by decomposition. He takes refuge in the backwoods, where he leads the life of solitude and isolation demanded by the disease of Lazarus. Mora takes on even more meaning for the people in his isolation, for he is now more than ever their suffering incarnated in the person of a man they consider holy. He embodies the physical and emotional isolation of every human being, but, with his disease, also the "unclean" and suffering race of his oppressed people:

Macario and his companions also came up against the sick man's determination to isolate himself, against his decision to stay where he was until the end.

"The dead don't mingle with the living . . ." he told Macario, speaking from a distance of several feet, and preventing them with a gesture from approaching any nearer. . . [my ellipsis].

He shook his head and looked at them with an unfathomable expression. It was as though a dead man had risen to testify to the irrevocability of death.

Then, to break the evil spell which seemed to have fallen upon them all, he sat down on the tree-trunk and began to play in farewell the Campamento Cerro León. This anonymous song of the Great War sounded more than usually lively and martial as it rose from the knotted strings of Gaspar's guitar.   "In face of that, there was nothing we could do," said Macario.

It must have seemed to them that the music sprang from the wild, dark land of magic. And in it they must have heard, especially Macario, the voice of innumerable, anonymous martyrdoms. (*H*, 21; ellipsis in text.)

It is in this painful isolation, which we can almost call "sacrificial" because of Mora's desire to quarantine himself from the people, that Gaspar Mora carves his figure of Christ. The anthropomorphic implications of this act are really of only a secondary importance. Gaspar Mora must have been well aware of the Christian tradition, and his creation of the figure of Christ is in keeping with the use of such images by Christians as reminders of the omnipresence of God and the redemptive powers of sacrificial suffering:

While he was in exile, he had carved it patiently, perhaps in order to have a companion which looked like a man, for solitude had become unbearable to him, much more terrible and degrading than his illness itself.

This was his gentle comrade.

Having survived him, it stood there peacefully. The pale wood was stained by his suppurating hands. He had made it on his own image. If a soul can take on a physical shape, then this was the soul of Gaspar Mora. (*H*, 24)

Macario says of the carving:

"it's a man who is speaking! We cannot understand God . . . but a man we can understand! . . . Gaspar is inside him! . . . There was something he wanted to tell us through this image of his. . . . When he knew that he would never come back, when he was already dead! . . ." (*H*, 27; ellipses in text.)

The townspeople accept the figure in the spirit in which it was made: as a symbol of the suffering of Christ as man and, hence, as a symbol of their own suffering. Their acceptance of this new image of Christ is spontaneous and overriding, despite the work of a heretic possessed by the devil.

Gaspar's message that can only be understood by his fellowmen, but not by the alien priest, is the fraternity of mankind in its common suffering incarnate in the Christ image. It is the image of a holy individual crucified, sacrificed as is man in his daily struggle for survival in a circumstance of total physical and spiritual oppression.

Their unspoken awareness of this truth is what brings Macario and the people to rebel against the sterile authority of the priest. Since the priest is unyielding in his refusal to accept the figure in the church, Macario and a few of the men construct a cross upon which to mount it. This shrine becomes famous overnight and the church is forced to recognize it. The wooden symbol of Mora's solitary death comes to articulate the anguish of his people. He had expressed a desire to leave a part of himself behind in order not to die forgotten. His last work is a transfiguration of his very soul, enshrined on the hill outside Itapé, the Kuimbaé-Rapé, the Road of Man: " 'For man, my children,' [Macario] said, repeating almost exactly what Gaspar had said, 'Man has two births. One when he is born, the other when he dies. . . . He dies, but he remains alive in others, if he has dealt kindly with his neighbors. If he has helped others during his lifetime, when he dies, the earth may devour his body, but his memory will live on . . .' " (H, 32; ellipses in text).

Mora's death is not the earthly end of his person. The figure of the son of man represents throughout the novel Roa's firm belief that there are outstanding individuals who are driven to find a way of expressing themselves even in death, an expression that, although it may not contribute materially to the welfare of a people mired for centuries in unrelenting enslavement, supports them spiritually and reinforces their belief in the common brotherhood of a suffering mankind. This is the central image of Son of Man, and the novel is insistent in developing the image as the affirmation of the necessity for the complete realization of man's obligation toward his people.

IV   Cristóbal Jara: the Fulfillment of the Figure

If Gaspar Mora represents the establishment of the Christ figure as the people see it, Cristóbal Jara is unquestionably the major embodiment of that figure in Son of Man. The prototypic rebel leader, Jara is presented from several perspectives in the central part of the novel. We are told in chapter 4 of his birth in the yerba mate plantations and of his escape with his parents while still a baby, fleeing the forced labor into which they have unwittingly sold themselves. This chapter is fittingly entitled "Exodus," and Roa is conscious of the need to give it a clearly biblical tone. By chapter 5 Jara has already become a strong rebel leader whose fame is based in part on the legends surrounding his parents' exodus. We learn in this chapter that Miguel Vera has been asked to provide the rebels with military training.

Although he is willing in principle, he betrays Jara duing a moment of drunkenness, Jara goes into hiding, and his band of men are ruthlessly destroyed by the authorities; Vera is sent to a prison camp, where he writes the diary that makes up chapter 7. In chapter 6 Jara is seen evading the authorities. He is eventually able to escape their pursuit, assisted by the lepers with whom he shares the status of a social outcast. Finally Jara reappears in chapter 8 as a soldier during the Chaco War, a war that successfully attracted broad national support and brought together as fellow combatents both rebels like Jara and traditional military supporters. In this chapter, "Mission," Jara is charged with the task of carrying water to the front line, where the troops are besieged without water. He undertakes the mission with a profound but unspoken sense of sacrificial zeal; he is killed as he approaches the lines by a stray bullet from the rifle of thirst-maddened Vera.

Throughout these chapters, which make up the bulk of the novel, there is a structural pairing between Vera and Jara, a pairing of which Vera is essentially unconscious, despite the fact that he is clearly the narrator of chapters 5 and 7. Jara, from his birth in the *yerbe mate* plantations—the living hell of the enslaved workers—to his self-sacrifice in order to bring water to his fellowmen, is again and again shown to be endowed with the Christly virtues established in the first chapter. By contrast Vera, both in his apparent sympathy with, but only partial understanding of, the rebels and in his eventual betrayal of them, comes across as a Judas figure who unwittingly destroys the Christ figure. Vera's betrayal is bipartite: it involves first the betrayal of the rebel movement, leading to Jara's persecution, and sub-sequently his unintentional shooting by Vera. Vera returns in the last chapter of the novel to discuss the plight of the Paraguayan people as the result of the destructive war. He either is unaware of his responsibility for Jara's death or does not consider that minor event of war worth mentioning. Yet the concluding note of his narrative, as he writes the final sentences prior to taking his own life, is one of unconscious irony: a sympathizer with armed popular revolution who nevertheless has unwittingly played the role of Judas vis-à-vis the novel's most significant son of man.

In the novel the Chaco War war—Paraguay was the "victor" in a national boundary dispute with Bolivia—is the major representation of the senseless suffering of the people in the name of a vacuous concept of the Paraguayan nation. The conflict takes place in the Chaco region, the wild backlands of Paraguay. Vera sees this area as

an *Edén maldito* ("an accursed Eden") in which man reverts under
the burden of the war to a subhuman atavism that threatens to destroy
him completely. Of course this atavism is the result of a war imposed
upon the people by their oppressors, and it becomes yet one more
eloquent representation of the suffering of the people: "In a few days
we have retrogressed thousands of years. Only a miracle can save us.
But in this accursed Eden no miracle is possible" (*H*, 179).

It is not difficult to see in Vera's words, so indicative of the frenzied
despair induced by the conditions of the war, a culmination of the
destructive tendencies of a putatively "civilized" society to which not
only Vera (in his weak way), Jara, and his rebel band are opposed, but
surely the author as well. The "War of Thirst," as the commander-in-
chief, Estigarribia, had called it (see *H*, 168), seems to be the final
embodiment of a national suicidal drive that threatens to destroy the
people.[7] This destruction is narrated in terms of the blind dedication
of Jara to his mission, a mission that leads irrevocably to his own
annihilation. For Vera the whole campaign is a manifestation of
human persecution, the projection of the oppression of his people
onto a noble and allegedly patriotic plane.

In the chapter entitled "Mission," which describes Jara's self-
sacrifice for his fellowmen, water signifies the plague of thirst. The
representation of the thirsty combatants and their reaction to the
sight of Jara's watertruck is credibly presented in strongly atavistic
terms. We quickly grasp what drives these men to the bestial struggle
to obtain life-sustaining water. Yet we also understand Jara and how
he is animated by the same impetus that has been the motivating
principle of his life of struggle against oppression. He is fully
conscious of the meaning that his life has and of the mission that he
senses, no matter how unconsciously, he is obligated to undertake for
his fellowmen. He is secure in the compelling belief that the salvation
of mankind rests with man, either as a vehicle of some unknown God
or as the initiator of the task of his own redemption:

"Do you believe in miracles, Cristóbal?"
"Miracles?"
"In impossible things happening? Things that only God can do?"
"What man can't do, no one can do," he said gruffly.
"Yes. . . . Perhaps that is the kind of strength which makes miracles
happen."
"I don't know. I don't understand words. I only know what I am capable of
doing. I have a mission. I am going to carry it out. That is all I know." (*H*, 221)

There is nothing epic about Jara, as his dialogue with his girl friend, a former prostitute, reveals. His function in the novel is not to fulfill the role of a superhero who will save his people. Rather, he is called upon to be one responsible individual among the countless many who will, working together, effect some good. It is important to remember that Jara is the figure of the son of man only to the extent that he represents many who fulfill a role analogous to his own. It is necessary to keep in mind the collective tradition that binds men to mankind and to see Jara as neither superman nor superhero. Perhaps for this reason his "mission" is such an insignificant one in the long run. But for the majority of mankind insignificance and oblivion are its lot, and not heroic martyrdom:

> Suddenly, when he was not thinking about them, he would see them again, deep, turbid, compelling, showing him the road, forcing him to go on. For now the only thing that mattered was to go on, always at all costs, through the wood, through the desert, through the merciless heat of the sun and the head of his dead friend, through this terrible country where life and death were indissolubly joined. That was his destiny. And what other destiny could there be for a man like Cristóbal Jara except to pursue the obsession which enslaved him along a narrow forest trail or over the limitless plain filled with the savage smell of freedom. To force his way through the inexorable thicket of facts, tearing his flesh against their thorns, but at the same time transforming them by the power of his will, which became all the stronger as he accepted the facts. "What man cannot do, no one can do . . ." he had said himself. And there were countless anonymous men like him. Their strength was not rooted in a simple faith in a law which included and transcended them. They knew nothing, perhaps not even what hope is. Nothing but this: to want something so much that everything else is forgotten. To go forward, forgetting themselves. Happiness, triumph, defeat, sex, love, despair, were nothing but stages of their journey through the boundless desert. One of them fell by the wayside, another carried on, leaving a track, a footprint, a drop of blood on the ancient crust of the earth. However small the traces they left behind, they were enough to fertilise the fierce, elemental virginity of the soil and to make flower again in those who came after their own purpose and determination. (*H*, 223; ellipses in text.)

The novel makes it explicitly clear that we do not have a narrative of impressive heroics. It is rather the attempt to express the "historic reality" of Paraguay common not only to the Paraguayan people, not only to the Latin American common man, but, lamentably, to the majority of mankind everywhere. What gives the monotony of life any transcendent importance is the altruism of a few men like Jara who, while they may not be able to bring about immediate social revolution and the redemption of the people from their degradation, can give it the dignity of their own persons and evoke for man the meaning of Mora's leprous Christ figure.

Roa Bastos has employed a diffuse narrative platform to construct his novel. Not only does this result in a wide panorama of events and personalities, but it prevents the stagnation of the thematic economy he strives for in his basically autonomous chapters, which are in turn divided into relatively brief fragments. At the same time, he is successful in presenting a sweeping analysis of the collective tradition of his country through the figurative son of man, the suffering Christ of mankind. The narrative progression of the novel details the emergence of the Christ of Itapé, the verification on both a personal and a collective level of the necessity for its existence, the reaffirmation of the suffering of the people by the representation of the Chaco War, and the sowing of the seeds—at least in Vera's mind—of an earnest and inevitable revolt. *Son of Man* expresses the firm conviction that the redemption of the Paraguayan people will be carried out by a responsible body of individuals who have as their goal the ultimate materialization of human dignity. In the words of Vera, for these men "the strength of the fellow-feeling between them is their God" (*H*, 248).

V   *Narrative Point of View in* Son of Man

The first impression from reading *Son of Man* is that the nine chapters are narrated exclusively by Miguel Vera, the ex-military officer who dies at the end of the ninth chapter and whose writings are discovered by Rosa Monzón and published by her in the hope that they will be of some use "now when the country is once again on the brink of civil war . . ." (*H*, 255).[8] The majority of those who have studied the novel have concluded that Vera is the only narrator and that, given Monzón's letter that closes the narrative, we are to understand the story related up to this point as a mélange of Vera's recollections, evocations, mental ramblings, written diaries, etc. Seymour Menton notes a certain variation in Vera's manner of presentation; yet he sees no problem in accepting him as the only narrator.[9] I myself had also maintained this position, considering Vera as the exclusive narrator (with the obvious exception of Monzón's letter, which provides us with certain already evident information concerning Vera's personality and the debilitating "romanticism" that afflicts him) in my earlier study on Roa Bastos's works.[10]

However, a new reading that attends to the overall sense of the individual chapters and their narrative mode indicates that this characterization of the novel's structure is inaccurate and that it is necessary to recognize that only half of the chapters are narrated by Vera and that the other half are narrated by some other voice or voices. That reason why many have come to the conclusion that Vera is the sole narrator is probably due to the fact that he is present in the novelistic action of most of the chapters. Thus he is not only a spectator-narrator but also a direct participant in the same events that he is detailing. Moreover, at some points he becomes the catalyst of the novelistic action, for example when he drunkenly betrays Jara and his revolutionary band (chapters 5–7), when he finds himself besieged without water in the Chaco and sends Jara for water (chapter 8), and when he provokes the hollow enthusiasm of the people upon the return to Itapé of an ex-soldier, a man who has been spiritually destroyed. The enthusiasm whipped up by Vera lays bare the hypocrisy of an official war that served the interests of the men in power at the expense of a citizenry only plunged deeper into poverty and despair (chapter 9).

Nevertheless despite Vera's direct participation and self-observation as an actor in some of the chapters, it is probable that only the odd-numbered chapters are narrated directly in Vera's voice. And with the exception of a reference to Vera and to his betrayal by the principal characters in the sixth chapter, Vera does not participate in the events related in chapters 2, 4, 6, and 8. In the first chapter, which establishes the historical as well as the "spiritual" context of the novel (see section III above), Vera tells us what he remembers about Macario, Gaspar Mora, and the Christ Mora carves. The Christ that now hangs from a cross put up on sacred ground on a hilltop on the outskirts of Itapé is unquestionably the recurring symbol of the book, as Vera himself observes in his initial attempts to interpret Mora and the Paraguayan people. It is a symbol both of man crucified, who must be avenged, and of the ecclesiastical Christ, who must be punished for his failure to comply with the promise to alleviate the suffering of mankind (see *H*, 13). In terms of the overall unity of the novel, the opening chapter establishes the unifying tone of a story of universal dimensions for the Paraguayan people. With respect to Vera, it is his best sentimental flight in the attempt to recreate what was in his eyes a decisive moment for a people that he is barely able to comprehend. Vera, of course is a typical Latin American (or third-world) figure: although a Paraguayan by birth and formation, he comes from a middle-class minority that has little profound contact with the mass of its fellow citizens and is fundamentally concerned with preserving its own precarious privileges.

Vera writes in the third chapter about his trip from Itapé to the military school he is to attend in Asunción. He travels with a servant from his father's household and with her sick baby; at night, Vera deprives the baby of its mother's milk by suckling at her breast himself. Vera narrates this incident without commentary in order to point out the first manifestations of his serious character weaknesses. For purposes of a connecting link between the chapters, one of the incidents of the third chapter concerns the Russian doctor, Dub-rovsky, whose story has already been presented in chapter 2. In chapter 5 Vera recalls his walk with Jara to the old train car where the revolutionary group that intends to ask Vera for military training is waiting for them. Almost the entire chapter is given over to the details of this walk. Vera tells us how he can still remember past events of the town, like the bombing of the revolutionaires of the generation of Jara's father. He recalls Jara's own parents, already legendary figures in the minds of the people, the Russian doctor (also legendary—or at least infamous—in his own mysterious way), and the leprosarium that the doctor had built and that could still be made out in the distance on the edge of the village. Vera walks a few steps behind Jara, and the latter's scarred back, graphic evidence of his repeated mistreatment at the hands of the authorities, serves to stimulate Vera's recollections.

In the seventh chapter, Vera provides by means of entries in a diary he is keeping the details of his stay at Peña Hermosa until the outbreak of the Chaco War, when he is besieged there without water. The use of the diary has the advantage of creating the illusion of an objective presentation of Vera's secret, personal nature, since the entries put down every couple of days constitute a trajectory that Vera, trapped in his obsessive self-concern, must have been unable to perceive, yet one that is readily apparent to the "outside" reader. This trajectory moves toward delirium and hallucination, conditions that once again serve to reveal to us the instability of the narrator's character. Although the casual reader will accept this illusion of the diary as reliable, there is at the very end of the series of entries something that destroys in large part any chance that we accept it as a text compiled on a day-to-day basis. At issue is the final entry wherein Vera describes in detail, at a time when he and his troops are at the breaking point over the lack of water, his own loss of consciousness at the precise moment that Jara arrives with the watertruck. The section is preceded by a date and has all the earmarks of a legitimate diary entry. But the final words, under the entry for September 29, describe something that Vera could not have written down at the same time it was happening to him: "Now the truck has appeared at the head of the trail. She is still tormenting me. Her tricks and ironies are endless. In a cloud of dust, its wheels on fire, the truck has come zigzagging through the clearing. I have fired several bursts at it too, a whole round without destroying this monster of my delirium. It is coming on, with its tank swaying and its wheels on fire, and bright fountains of water springing from its side. Now it has crashed into a tree. It is here. . . . It is summoning me . . ." (*H,* 182; ellipses in text).

One assumes that Vera faints at this moment, unaware that he has in effect destroyed the watertruck and wasted much of its precious cargo—and unaware that he has also killed Jara. Vera's killing of Jara, it should be noted, is one of Roa's major ironies in the novel. An inevitable resolution of the antagonic values that Vera and Jara embody, the betrayal is distributed over two major segments of the novel: chapter 5, in which Vera denounces the ragtaggle band of revolutionaries he has agreed to train, and chapter 7, with the portrayal of the meaningless Chaco War that brings the two together in the presumed common national cause. In this final resolution of a symbolic binary antagonism that results in the destruction of one value figure by another, the irony lies precisely in the fact that only the reader can be aware of what has occurred. Thus while all of the other entries are presumably legitimate and therefore reliable, this last entry must have been written and included along with the others at a later moment, when Vera would have been more able to recall so completely—or to imagine so completely—this last day of his military career. If the entry was composed at a time later than September 29 and if Vera has learned that his delirious bursts of machine-gun fire have finally put an end to Jara's life, his text gives no indication of it.

The ninth chapter, as has already been noted, refers to the return of an ex-combatant and the shock that he and other demented returning "warriors" have on Vera's fertile imagination. Although the final words before his death may be an expression of Roa Bastos's own profound feelings (that is, the need for popular uprisings and for an

eventual and total revolution), they are also excellent evidence of
Vera's tendency to romanticize, to sentimentalize, to convert everything into an overflowing emotionalism that, in its cathartic effect,
only inhibits serious action. One should examine, for example, his
evocation of what the future holds for Paraguay (*H*, 247–48). What
Vera says is undoubtedly true, but it is the fever-pitched emotion
with which it is said that is what attracts our attention as revealing of
Vera.

In contrast to the odd-numbered chapters, the even-numbered
ones not only do not include Vera as a participant, but are concerned
with events at times and in places where it would have been difficult,
if not impossible, for Vera to be present. One could say that the fact
that Vera does not appear as a participant in the even-numbered
chapters is not in itself important. Either Vera has become more
controlled vis-à-vis his own self-obsession, choosing to restrain the
egoism that stands out in the odd-numbered chapters, or what we
have is Vera writing the even-numbered chapters as the result of later
investigations made to fill in the gaps of his own memory. What is
certain is that chapters 2, 4, 6, and 8, as opposed to those of the other
five, relate events that Vera really could not have observed directly.
The narrative action of chapter 2, dedicated to the Russian doctor,
takes place while Vera is in a military school in Asunción: Vera in
chapter 3 has only seen Dubrovsky thrown off the train in Sapukai.
The events in chapter 2 take place subsequent to the doctor's
detrainment.

The fourth chapter, which concerns Jara's parents and their life in
the *yerba mate* fields of the Alto Paraná, involves a period that falls
either before Vera's birth or shortly after. Since Vera is about Jara's
age (there is about an eight-year difference; Vera is the older one), the
latter having been born a little before the legendary biblical exodus of
his parents from their bondage in the immense fields owned by a
foreign concern, we are safe in insisting that any narrative by Vera
could only be the result of a reconstruction on the basis of what others
told him. And here we have a significant problem. It is not just that
Vera could not have played a role in the events of chapter 4—his
investigations and inquiries much later could have provided
memories of the events to reconstruct the story. What is more
important is the fact that it is quite improbable that Vera would have
been able to reconstruct to a sufficient degree the lives of Natí and
Casiano in Tukurú-Pukú. From where would he have gotten the
facts? Surely not from the parents, who had already died when in the

fifth chapter Vera is in Sapukai, having just been expelled from military school. And surely not from Cristóbal Jara, who communicates more with gestures than with words. Although the story of the parents had become myth in Sapukai, the myths of the people are based on conflict and values and do not record enough necessary detail to enable Vera to re-create plausibly the life on the *yerba mate* plantations. Of course one possibility is that Vera takes the vague popular myths and creates a story as though it were reconstructed fact. Yet, as in the case of his diary and his final letter, we would expect internal evidence of Vera's romantic, pseudomythic fantasizing, and we have, as best as can be discovered, none at all.

Nor can the sixth chapter be by Vera. When he betrays Jara and his men, he is sent to the Peña Hermosa penal colony, where he is held until the outbreak of the Chaco War. Once again, investigations after the war could have provided him with the material for completing the story, which in this case has to do with Jara's luck after the betrayal (he is the only one to survive the careful extermination of the betrayed revolutionaries by the government). But when one recalls that Vera dies about a year after the war, he could not practically speaking have had time to undertake the inquiries necessary to compose the chapters, nor even time to fabricate them. A tempting hypothesis is that Vera wrote the even-numbered chapters, but on the basis of pure fantasy in an effort to imagine what had to have happened, given the myth or the result of what did occur. Yet given ths sense of the work and, as will be discussed in a moment, the importance of the even-numbered chapters, it is impossible to believe that such is the case. The function of the chapters that Vera could not have written is so important in their presentation of Roa Bastos's own presumed vision of the power of the Paraguayan people, that the impressive meaning of the novel would be unclear if one had to accept the idea that these chapters were simply the product of the romantic imagination of this weak human being. By the same token, any insistence that they must nevertheless be attributed to Vera should be accompanied by a new interpretation whereby the chapters "imagined" by Vera in his fertile fantasy—as opposed to those chapters that do not pretend to be anything other than his sentimental memories—can take on a new transcendent meaning in the overall structure of *Son of Man.*

And if the foregoing were not sufficient to prove that Vera does not narrate the even-numbered chapters, we have also a few other characteristics of the novel that support our contention. For example, if Gaspar Mora and Cristóbal Jara are the two Christological figures in the novel, one contemplative and the other active, why are they so different in their human dimension? That is, where Jara is a man of flesh and blood in chapters 6 and 8, a man of a certain quiet heroism or, better, of a quiet inner power, Mora who has already died when the young Vera remembers Macario in the first chapter, comes off as a cardboard figure, and completely romanticized and completely mythic. Part of the reason for this contrast in presentation lies in the fact that Mora was already dead and had already been converted into a myth. But part of the reason also lies in the fact that Vera recalls what Macario tells in his senility. *But this is not enough because Vera, who speaks, could have restored the figure of Mora to a believable human dimension.* Nevertheless he chooses to accept the romantic— senile—version of Macario, who is the unconscious mythic voice of the people in his evocation of the entire Paraguayan prehistory. Mora is romanticized because he is a myth already and because Vera likes myths, especially sentimental ones that touch a basic sensitivity in his personality. Hence his musings in the first chapter as to what the Christ carved by Mora means, why it had been taken over by the people with such spontaneity, why the mysterious ritual continues to be celebrated every Good Friday, a "ceremony which gave to us villagers of Itapé the name of fanatics and heretics" (*H*, 9). Yet, these musings are often almost patronizing in tone.

There is also a great amount of stylistic variation between the even- and the odd-numbered chapters. The latter—Vera's own excited recollections—are often more than somewhat sentimental, some- what romantic, somewhat hyperbolic; the presence of Vera as a participant reduces them to the same level at which this incapacitated and spiritually lame romantic, as Rosa Monzón calls him, functions. The style of the even-numbered chapters, by contrast, is of biblical dimensions, and the narrative attempts to capture the transcendental sense of great human undertakings that, no matter how trivial they may be, reveal the power of the soul to survive its immediate, degrading circumstance. The Russian, Jara's parents, Jara himself are all figures endowed with a strength of personality that Vera could not have fully understood, much less represented with the deper- sonalized biblical style of the even-numbered chapters.

Although the matter deserves a detailed study before we can say unequivocally that it is indeed the case, I suggest that there is a significant difference between Vera's sentimental style in chapters 1, 3, 5, 7, and 9, and the biblical-mythic style of chapters 2, 4, 6, and 8. And this difference, in effect, supports the relative importance of the latter when compared with the chapters narrated by Vera. It is in the even-numbered chapters where man is portrayed in terms of the most radical possibilities of his being: the doctor's struggle with Good and Evil, both equally powerful, and his ultimate destruction by that struggle; the unheard of and decisive decision of Jara's parents in the face of a reality they can no longer withstand because it is robbing them of their dignity as human beings, a dignity revindicated in their exodus; the fraternity of suffering men that permits the salvation of Jara, already surrounded by the halo of a saint for the dignity he has inherited from his parents; and, finally, the strength of spirit, enclosed within Jara's weak and mortified body, in carrying out what he has accepted as his mission toward his fellowmen. There is unquestionably a contrast between these chapters and the ones attributable to Vera. Except for the first chapter, which, however sentimental it may be, has a greater importance for establishing the context for the entire novel, the other four odd-numbered chapters stand out for the lack of the "grandeur" or "greatness" that emerges from the even-numbered chapters. In effect, these chapters (3, 5, 7, and 9), have been called "transitional" as one way of underlining how antithetical they are in comparison with 2, 4, 6, and 8.

One function for this contrapuntal alternation between Vera and another unnamed narrator is not too difficult to propose: it underlines the grandeur of mankind, of the human individual—at least those who cluster around the figure of Jara—and, by contrast, the spiritual bankruptcy of sentimental and romantic types like Vera. The latter not only are incapable of understanding the Jaras but also in the end betray them in their own meanness of character. But then one could ask about the identity of this second narrator. Although it has been suggested that it could be another, "objective" side of Vera's character, this is highly unlikely. It is not necessary that the voice be identified with any of the "historical" participants in the novel's action. Rather we could say simply that it is Roa Bastos himself, speaking in his own voice (rather than through Vera's, as we have suggested he is doing in the closing pages of the latter's diary). The novel would thus be seen as providing the reader with a fundamentally significant contrast—and conflict—between the two points of view that are woven together throughout the novel via the alternating chapters. Or if one prefers a loftier assessment, we can say that it is "Christ" himself or another God that the reader could accept, with the point once again being our perception of the difference between a truly mythic narrative point of view and the pitifully inadequate point of view of someone like Miguel Vera. Whichever hypothesis prevails, it cannot in the last analysis fail to stress once again the importance of *Son of Man* as one of the most important and best elaborated novelistic documents of contemporary Latin American literature.

It is necessary for us now to turn to the importance of the narrative structure of *Son of Man* as we have described it thus far. We can begin by observing Roa's apparently dual goal in structuring his novel. On the one hand, he would have wanted to portray a particular stance in the face of the reality, both diachronic and synchronic, of his native country—its "intrahistory" as Rodríguez Alcalá has called it.[11] This stance extends to a perception of the burning need for "something to be done" to break the desperate cycle of oppression and the degradation of human dignity that has been Paraguay's inescapable lot. From this goal flows the historic unity of the novel, its social denunciation of the life on the *yerba mate* plantations, the stupidity of Paraguay's wars, the unconscious legacy of Dr. Francia embodied in the terror that serves as the common denominator of the people's existence. By the same token, we have also his focusing on certain human types, in particular on Gaspar Mora and Cristóbal Jara, in order to suggest the personality, the silent commitment with humanity, which must be possessed by those who would offer themselves to the task of renovating socially and morally the bases of Paraguayan life.

On the other hand, the fictional vision of Roa's novel concentrates on nothing less than the ethical-moral problem of that renovation. Miguel Vera crystallizes this problem in a personality that we come to know either through direct characterization (his own words, for example, at the end of the third part) or by means of the function of his narrative voice as we have interpreted it in our preceding commentary. Miguel Vera embodies the moral problem in an emphatic way precisely because he gives every indication of being committed to the renovation of Paraguayan society, despite his own personal roots. But yet it is obvious that he is incredibly lacking in sufficient strength of character to contribute to the urgent undertaking of the Cristóbal Jaras. What seems to occur inexorably is that this fatal conjunction of sentimental idealism and moral weakness degenerates into the cheap romanticism about which we have already spoken. The romanticism from which Vera suffers, in almost a pathological sense, is just as dangerous as the enemy himself, and hence Vera's almost unconscious and unwitting betrayal.

Roa's novel, then, sets itself the double goal of elaborating not only a sympathetic identification with the new Christs, men who will free the Latin American people from their enslavement by the modern Pharaohs, but also of showing how one of the reasons for the failures of the new Christs lies in the character of the Veras, who believe that their superficial verbal commitment, with none of the true suffering and sacrifice of the body, is sufficient. It would be tempting to see in Vera a mask, a persona, of the author himself or to want to measure Roa's own commitment against Vera's blunderings. Or to extract from Vera's writing a mea culpa of the novelist unable to play the role of a Jara in the vindication of his countrymen. Perhaps all of these possibilities are germane to an explanation of why his work manifests such a high degree of expressive tension and emotion. Nevertheless, when the critic sets out to discover these motivations, which are extrinsic to the narrative itself, he is attempting more to characterize Roa rather than the novel he wrote. To say that Vera was a writer who suffered from the disabling sentimentalism often attributed to the writer-intellectual is not the same thing as saying that Vera is nothing more or less than Roa Bastos's alter ego. In effect, the same alternation of chapters told by Vera with the chapters told by an unidentified narrative voice could be used to insist that the latter are the ones that are more "in character" for Roa Bastos the man, unyielding in his denunciation of the pernicious Veras.[12]

VI *Conclusions*

Roa Bastos in *Son of Man* attempts to find a solution for one of the most basic rhetorical difficulties of the novel: how to suggest an authorial stance toward the material being narrated, how to provide the reader with a concrete enough specification of the narrative in order to reach the "appropriate" conclusions desired by the author.[13] By making use of the alternation of narrative voices and by providing the previously discussed double characterization of Vera (that is, his own autobiographic commentaries versus his strikingly inappropriate sentimentalism), the novelist makes us enter into a significant segment of his ethical-moral problem. We can perceive clearly, if we grasp the subtlety of the change of narrative focus from the even-numbered to the odd-numbered chapters, the profound difference that exists between the sentimental and dangerously ineffective tone of Vera's chapters and the quasi-biblical tone that evokes the somber and powerful silences of the people incarnate in the person of Cristóbal Jara.

For the foregoing reasons one of Vera's last observations concerning his relations with the revolutionaries takes on even more
meaning, essentially ironic vis-à-vis Vera himself. Not only is his
comment pathetic; it bespeaks as well all of the irony of Vera's
marginal and ultimately antagonistic position toward the movement.
One could even say that Vera is more aware here of what he really
stands for than are revolutionarieis themselves, and for this reason he
chooses suicide, as much in order to free himself of the burden of his
responsibility for past failures as to save the revolutionaries from one
more betrayal at the hands of his kind:

So I go on with the pretence of being alive. I am only interested in the past.
The future means nothing to me . . . [my ellipsis]. But for these men around
me now, it is only the future which counts, for they see it is an extension of the
fascinating antiquity of the past. They never think of death. They live for
action, take each moment as it comes, and escape from themselves by
identifying themselves wholeheartedly with a cause, whether true, or false, it
does not matter. . . . They know no other way of living. For them, death does
not exist. They know that to admit its existence brings about disintegration
and dissolution. They just get on with living. Even Crisanto Villalba's
madness is a devouring passion like life itself [Villalba is the demented
excombatant returned from the Chaco War]. These men's thirst for life acts as
a compass through the thirstiest, most mysterious and most boundless desert
of all: the human heart. The strength of the fellow-feeling between them is
their God, they may crush it, break it, shatter it, but the pieces join together
again, and it is livelier and stronger than ever. And it moves in an
ever-widening spiral . . . [my ellipsis].
  Things must change. It is impossible to go on oppressing a nation
indefinitely. "Man is like a river, my sons . . ." said old Macario Francia, "a
river which is fed by other rivers, and which in turn feeds them. It is a bad
river which ends up in a bog. . . ." Stagnant water is poisonous. It breeds
malignant fevers which cause madness. Then, to cure the invalid or quiet
him, you have to kill him. This country is already overpopulated with graves.
"Harvests don't grow from corpses!"
  I am afraid that one day one of the rebels will come to me and ask me, as
once before in Sapukai, to teach them to fight. *I* teach them . . . how
ridiculous! But they don't need to be taught now. They have learned a lot.
Cristóbal Jara's truck did not cross the frontiers of death to save a traitor's life.
Enveloped in flames, it is still rolling on through the night, over the desert,
along the trains, bringing water to the thirsty survivors. (*H*, 248–49; ellipses
in text.)

CHAPTER 4

Recent Short Fiction

I *Introduction*

IN the terms of the literary production of best-selling authors like
Fuentes, Cortázar, and García Márquez, the public acclaim and
the quantity of writings produced by Roa Bastos since *Son of Man*
must be considered scant. Although Roa has attracted considerable
attention with his most recent novel, less than two dozen stories have
been published during the twenty-five years since *Thunder Among
the Leaves* (1953).[1] There can be little doubt that literary composition
is for Roa a painstaking process. It is in this context that we must
examine a short-story production that barely averages one a year: all
are excellent contributions to the genre in Latin America, and none
can legitimately be overlooked, although we will in fact limit
ourselves to analyzing only a few.

Alongside the stories included in *Thunder Among the Leaves,* the
stories presented in four recent collections,[2] which overlap to an
enormous degree, represent a tripartite artistic advancement.

The early stories are characterized by a tone that could well be
called "poetic" and could be identified with a neo-impressionism in
prose writing found more in vanguardistic literature of the twenties
or thirties than in post–World War II prose. If a deliberately prosaic
style of a Hemingway characterizes the latter period, the attempt to
fuse prose and poetry after the fashion of James Joyce seem more
indicative of the former. Whether the self-consciously poetic tone of
Roa's early stories is to be attributed to a slower artistic maturity in
Paraguay or to the writer's transition from imitations of baroque
Spanish poets to a prose inspired by both myth and socialist realism is
a moot question. Certainly the choice of prose style was calculated on
Roa's part. In the case of someone of such obvious superiority over
other Paraguayan writers, we must assume his extensive familiarity
with mid-twentieth-century prose fiction. It is less of a moot question

whether his deliberate choice of prose style can be identified with a
desire to go beyond facile forms of socialist realism, which had pretty
well exhausted the potential of its orthodox aesthetic principles by
1950,[3] and to show that serious statements could be made concerning
the collective reality of a people within a highly poeticized context.
Needless to say, more recent Latin American fiction has validated the
underlying assumption attributed to Roa in these stories, as least as
far as a highly self-conscious literary format is concerned. This is
particularly notable when one places Cortázar and Sabato's inventive
but none the less "committed" fictions alongside the neo-socialist
realism of David Viñas.[4]

In the stories that I am about to consider, Roa has continued to
adhere to a belief in the productive combination of an unmistakable
political commitment and a foregrounded literary structure, and the
reader will find that a complex rhetorical structure appears in the
place of the earlier poeticized language. By "rhetorical structure" I do
not mean simply the presence of an overt structure, since all
literature is by definition characterized by an underlying, organizing
structure. Rather what is meant is a certain experimentation with
modes of fictional presentation, the attempt to discover the proper
"angle" of development for the story in order best to achieve
artist-reader communication (something that has often been called
the "pragmatics" of literature).[5] Nowhere will this be more evident
than in the extremely perplexing story, "Borrador de un informe"
("Draft of a Report").

With the unmistakably lyrical quality of the earlier stories came
also an almost inevitable degree of sentimentality. It was due not so
much to the author's maudlin identification with his suffering coun-
tryman and the complex stagnation of their existence, but rather
more to an overidealization of the characters that embody his mythic
perceptions. Nowhere is this more evident than in the evocation of
pseudo-Christ figures, especially in the title story. Third-world
literature—and, indeed, orthodox socialist realism—can easily suc-
cumb to such a form of sentimentality. Where the writer is concerned
with portraying the "alternate" humanity of people who inhabit
alledged backwaters of civilization, there is a marked tendency
toward overidealization. This is the case with cheapened forms of
Latin American folklorism, like the commerical manifestations of Río
de la Plata gauchesque traditions or of Mexican revolutionary sentiment, 1910 vintage. In a writer like Colombia's García Márquez,
given over to portraying a remote society called Macondo, barely

accessible to the routes of the modern, outside world and a micro-cosm of centuries of Latin American provincial "solitude," the tendency toward sentimentality could have been irresistible. Yet García Márquez solves the problem of sentimentality by adopting a tone of mordant irony toward human weaknesses that is nevertheless also a loving humor toward what is redemptive in man. The result is some of the most sophisticated yet entertaining—and not at all sentimental—fiction in Latin America. João Guimarães Rosa, on the other hand (and like Guillermo Cabrera Infante, who could have sentimentalized his portrait of pre-Castro Havana in *Tres tristes tigres* [*Three Trapped Tigers*]), finds the solution in a complex linguistic expressionism (surrealism for some critics) that achieves enough alienation to prevent sentimentality and to encourage, instead, an intellectualized understanding.

In Roa's stories written since 1953, some sentimentality may be noted in pieces like "El baldío" ("The Vacant Lot"), where negative human emotion is replaced by a positive behavior that, if not clearly religious in the sense of suggesting the power of Christian beliefs, at least uses implied religious metaphors. Such a metaphoric procedure has been a constant in Roa's fiction. Nevertheless, once the author decides to make use of complex structures such as we find in "Draft of a Report," he moves away from sentimentality toward a more intellectualized reader comprehension. We have seen how Roa attempted in *Son of Man* to negate the validity of Vera's sentimental-ity, which is shown to be an important emotion. In one sense, of course, Vera is one alter ego of the author, haunted by a facile lachrymosity that must be overcome in order to make way for more valid forms of identification with mankind.

The foregoing observations concerning sentimentality and the overly facile reader identification which it encourages holds true for the more specialized case of sociopolitical commitment. It is one thing for a writer to identify himself with a particular position and yet quite another for him to give it adequate artistic representation. In this regard, vague ethical judgments such as "sincerity," "depth of feeling," "personal involvement," and so on will simply not suffice, for no one has yet convincingly demonstrated how the critic is to correlate an author's extra literary sincerity with the objective qualities of his work. The work become autonomous from its author and must be measured in terms of its own objective qualities. By the same token only Eric Hoffer's "true believer" (something Roa refuses to be) conceives of reality, political or otherwise, in terms of black and white, and one of the hallmarks of the truly revolutionary writer is the acutely critical stance that prevents an antirevolutionary stagnation of any one doctrinaire position. One can adhere to well-defined political beliefs that are obvious to all but the most uninformed reader. But this does not simplify the literary expression of the ambiguities of man's adherence to specific beliefs, his weaknesses and his vacillations, as well as his corruption by both the enemies of those beliefs and by the very nature of "true believing" itself. This is why, despite the acceptance by most of his readers of Roa's conviction that Paraguay is a truly tragic nation (an example of Lévi-Strauss's *tristes tropiques*),[6] subject to the cruelest of exploitations and the destruction of human dignity, a story like "Thunder Among the Leaves" ultimately rings false. This is because it sentimentalizes both character and action. Part of this sentimentalization—which comes off as a ringing pronouncement of prophetic redemption—is the portrayal of a moral-ethical ideal of political action without the shadings provided by an inquiry into what human behavior is really like in the face of such an ideal. Man may firmly hold ideals and yet behave in a profoundly ambiguous manner toward them; he may even come to betray those ideals unwillingly and perhaps unknowingly. Such is a fundamental fact of human nature that has not yet, regrettably, been proven to be noninherent, and it is by choosing to ignore this circumstance that a literature rings false if it portrays human behavior in terms of correct ideals as utopian or assumes that, by adhering to those ideals, human behavior will be unambiguous.

In *Son of Man* Roa Bastos, as a writer, is undecided about accepting this ambiguity. He appears to sentimentalize Cristóbal Jara rather unremittingly, while the weaknesses of an "intellectual revolutionary" like Miguel Vera are given an amply critical portrayal. It remains to be seen to what degree Roa captures in his recent stories the ambiguity of human behavior, whether in terms of the character's own conscious involvement. One thing we may be sure of: readers recognize an undeniable correlation between the complexity of a literary work and the complexity of human experience that an author accepts. Put differently, it is no accident that a highly objective, often hermetic form of fiction has emerged among a group of revolutionary Latin American writers for whom human behavior is indeed a murky, ambiguous, and complex matter. Witness the way in which his ambiguity is treated by one of the patriarchs of Latin American revolutionary writers, Alejo Carpentier, in his *El siglo de las luces* (1959; translated as *Explosion in a Cathedral*). Set in the eighteenth century, *Explosion in a Cathedral* examines the "fortunes" and vicissitudes of the French revolution when transplanted to the Caribbean and subsequently corrupted by ambiguous human nature. This nature is not easily portrayed via a literature indulging in facile or persuasively utopian prophecies of a better social order that remains, quite unfortunately but also quite inescapably, a most distant ideal. In the face of this circumstance, and in the face of the unusually acute tragedy of Paraguay it would be easy for a revolutionary writer simply to lapse into bitter cynicism. This has, in fact, been the case with Gabriel Casaccia, a writer of undeniable but misspent talent. Roa, in turning to more complex narrative forms, has discovered alternate ways of reconciling an unrelentingly harsh reality with an unyielding personal ethic.

II "Moriencia": Cowardliness and Collective Falsification

An exceptional example of the qualities of Roa's recent fiction is "Moriencia" ("Slaughter"), part of a group of five pieces written in 1967.[7] The title is a neologism based on the verb *morir*, "to die," and connotes something like "slaughter" or "massacre." The use of the word in the text has a major symbolic importance, but less for what it connotes than for the context in which it is used. This fact is mentioned from the outset in order to show that what is of greater significance in the story is the context in which the slaughter of rebellious villagers is recalled than the betrayal that produces it.

One might read "slaughter" superficially as the narrator's chance recollection of Chepé Bolívar, his tragic act of cowardliness and the ensuing bloody repression by government forces. The narrator overhears Chepé mentioned by an old lady on the *mixto* (a combined passenger and freight train). Interested, he inquires after her knowledge of the legendary villager and receives as a reply a version of Chepé's involvement in the ill-fated rebellion that does not correspond to his own. Chepé is for the old woman a hero who refused to obey to order to send the telegraphic warning of ambush to the government troops. For the narrator—and it is significant that he is younger and apparently "educated"—Chepé supposedly did fail to send the betraying message, not because of any courageousness but out of a paralyzing cowardliness. In the latter version. Chepé lived the rest of his life haunted by his weakness in the face of the demand for his collaboration. Thus the story can be understood in terms of cowardliness versus noble endeavors, a cowardliness not of the evil, but of the weak. The latter may have a noble conviction, but they lack the strength to support the cause of the righteous. Yet Roa's tone is not one of indignation. Chepé (the versions of the two "reporters" seem to agree in this) lived the last years of his life haunted by his behavior in the crucial test put to his soul, laboriously making and refinishing his own coffin, like some mythological figure condemned forever to weave, unravel, and reweave his own shroud. Chepé, at least in the young narrator's eyes, is a tragic figure who dearly pays for his cowardliness:

> When Chepé could no longer move, the teacher would go to his house to give him a hand with the work. The coffin had been completed for some time. But between the two of them some detail was always being found that needed retouching or finishing. Like a canoe, that coffin, like the teacher Cristaldo's own canoe. Perhaps even better, of greater quality, more resistent, with better lines. First class for going up river to its sources, like the teacher wanted to do, but he could only float around in the lagoon. His old dug-out leaked all over the place.
> The letters on the far-ends of Chepé's coffin had been carved there by the teacher, one by one, with the point of a knife. Prison labor. Imagine another string of years for it. . . . *There is nothing but the beginning and what comes before the beginning.* . . . What did that mean? A message? A dedication? Flattery from two fading old men.[8]

On a deeper level, however, the story is more concerned with the narrator's preoccupation over what he sees as the inaccuracies of the old woman's story. He alleges at one point that she is only repeating what she has been told and not what she knows—or could know—firsthand: "The secondhand dealer was remembering that. She was telling a story that had been told to her" (*M*, 13). On the other hand, the narrator, who admits that the events at issue go back many years, confesses that he too may not be completely correct in his disagreements with the old woman: "Maybe that's not the way it is, maybe my memory is betraying me too" (*M*, 14). One's first impression is that Roa is suggesting the frailty of memory, even when what is at stake is something as important as the bloody repression of a peasant uprising. Yet if an interplay between the two versions of events were meant to evoke a commonplace concerning the illusions of truth and the relativity of human emotions, a superior point of view would serve better to contrast two equally valid and two equally invalid versions. Why does the young man narrate, thus allowing his version ostensibly to dominate (although an ironic impact derives

from allowing the old woman's words to close the text)? And why such
concern anyway over the accuracy of his own version?

One must recall that the crux of disagreement is that Chepé is for
the narrator a pathetic coward, while for the old woman he is a hero.
Thus the structure of the story takes the basic form of "not A, but B," a
venerable rhetorical figure of diction used for purposes of contrast.
We are shown throughout that is was *not* as the woman remembers,
but as the narrator remembers. In this way there is an underlying
polarity between segments of one paragraph or between two paragraphs, where two successive units of the narrative are devoted to
conflicting recollections. One should note the ironic use of the word
"chortled" with reference to the woman and the very explicit *no* with
which the narrator announces his own version; also that here, as
throughout, he keeps his contradiction to himself:

"Tall, dark, slow, with bird's feet. Always wearing a *poncho* [type of cloak] in
winter and in summer. At night when there was a moon he would stick on a
floppy hat and on top of that he would cover himself with a woman's parasol.
He'd go out walking, frightening people. How couldn't I know him" the
secondhand dealer chortled. "No, why he scarcely left his hut," I con-
tradicted her in my thoughts. Naked, his blisters greased with sweat, he was
so thin. He'd remain inside, working with wood of his coffin by the light of a
candle. From far off in the night you could hear the blows of the adze and the
chisel of the tree trunk. "There's Chepé sending another telegram," I can
remember us saying in town when we could hear that underground tapping
of a woodpecker. (*M*, 11).

This sort of counterpoint continues through at least a half dozen
major points having to do with the one defining act of Chepé's life and
its consequences. In each case, we hear the woman speaking as
though oblivious of the presence of her interlocutor, while the
narrator limits himself (or is it that he simply resigns himself?) to
contradicting her in his thoughts. It would seem that verbalization of
his version is out of place. Not only is it likely that the woman would
not heed him, but "Of what use would it have been for me to argue?
After all, what happened can never be taken care of by words" (*M*,
14).

Yet, once again, why does the narrator appear, in fact, to be so
concerned with the discrepancies of memory? Of course, in the first
place, he is truly interested in hearing about Chepé, and it is certain
that the old man, forever working and reworking his coffin, was a
vivid childhood memory, much like Gaspar Mora in the first chapter

of *Son of Man*. One way of understanding the narrator's consternation is to set aside the interest in Chepé as a particular Judas figure and to stress the pathetic irony that lies behind the old woman's distorted and indeed falsified version. Not only has the collective memory apparently misunderstood Chepé's motives. It has, in a process that must attach some emotional significance to what remains latent in the mind, converted him into a hero. We must insist that the narrator's version is the most accurate (at one point near the end of the story, he reports Chepé's confession of weakness and states that his failure to carry out the order was not heroism, but resulted from an immobilizing fear [*M*, 15]) and that the story should not be seen as an example of the relativity of truth.

Of course, the truth is relative in terms of the personally held versions of the two characters. But it is not relative vis-à-vis the reader, and, as a consequence, vis-à-vis the implied author. That the narrator "controls" the story and that there is an absence of any device that would weaken or ironize his point of view insures our willingness to "take his side" in the unspoken dispute. What, then, emerges as most important is not the cowardliness itself, but the circumstance by which it has been transformed into a heroic deed. We are not really told the process by which this happens. Rather, we are expected to sense its implications: the process involves a gradual loss of detail under the burden of advancing years, both the woman's age and the advance of historical time. It is also the result of the superimposition of one defective recollection upon another. Thus at one point the narrator insists that the woman is remembering what she has been told, not what she knew firsthand. And to this it is possible to add the suggestion of a deliberately propagated "official version."

The impact of this circumstance for the reader is a critical attitude toward the romantic notion that the people will not forget the injustices done them, that they will preserve in their collective memory the bloody *moriencias* committed against them, and that they will, in time, take their collective retribution.[9] Ironically it is the old woman who uses the word *moriencia*, but she no longer seems able to remember what it should connote. In fact, she appears not even to be sure which *moriencia* was involved out of the innumerable ones that have served as punctuation points in the peasants' struggle for justice. Thus, she confuses the events of the insurrection in which Chepé played a part with the insurrection of Sapukai described in *Son of Man*, when a train loaded with explosives was sent to destroy the rebel-held station. Far from being a voice of the collective unconscious that carries within its depths the accumulated memory of injustice and the seeds of successful rebellion, the old woman is the mouthpiece of a collective oblivion, of a collective confusion, of a collective unconsciousness. Why this should be so is not made clear, and in the absence of any clarification there is the temptation to attribute any chance of productive anger to the narrator and his "correct" memory.

Yet, as we have seen, he is resigned to the ineffectualness of disputing the old woman's story and to the possibility that his own memory may be equally defective. In short, if the woman is the pathetic embodiment of the illusion of an indignant collective unconsciousness of the people, her garbled version, the product of Lévi-Strauss's mythopoeic "savage mind" (*pensée sauvage*), the narrator is another one of Roa's romantically helpless intellectuals for whom writing and the denunciation of the savage mind is a form of expiating their resignation to an ultimate dead end. In this context, allowing the text to end with the old woman's final, false version is doubly ironic, since both her story and what she embodies have, so to speak, the last word over the supposedly controlling narrator: " 'We buried him in that coffin,' the secondhand dealer said. 'But not in the cemetery. The procession could not get through the shooting that surrounded the village, and we had to bury him in a pasture. Despite the bullets that whistled overhead, no one missed the procession for that dead man to whom the oldest of us owed our lives' " (*M*, 16).

After these words and the open-ended fashion in which they conclude the text (for example, one cannot help but envision the narrator's unspoken and unreported "correction" of these words), it is unnecessary to insist on how removed this story is from denunciatory testimonials. Yet "Slaughter" is none the less effective for its use of a contrapuntal structure and its articulation of a critical attitude toward the false romanticizing of a simply, revolutionary collective unconsciousness among the common people. The human mind is, regrettably, too frail an instrument for such a noble illusion.

III *"Cuerpo presente": Death and Eternal Return*

The five stories dated 1967 constitute a thematic unit; indeed, one critic has stressed the recurrence of characters (Chepé Bolívar and the enigmatic schoolteacher who aids the latter in carving his coffin) and situations (a popular uprising, brutally extinguished by government troops). To these qualities we add a third, one perhaps more significant than the continuity of characters and situation: the first-person, participant narrator. Although it is difficult to be certain about it, the narrator in four of the five pieces appears to be the same man, who recalls past events with a focus that alternates between what he could have perceived as a child and what he can now say about childhood events as an adult. In "Nonato" ("Unborn"),[10] the first-person narrative voice belongs to a child who has reached the decision to drown himself in order to leave his mother free to remember her dead husband (the drowning is symbolic: if the title is taken literally, the child is "not born," and is still being carried by the mother as a constant burden that reminds her of the husband who is now gone; thus, the child's "drowning" means that he will be stillborn). We only see the child's perceptions and his monologue, which he can neither verbalize nor interpret after the fact, as can an adult who looks back and understands from the vantage point of age events and feelings of his youth. Yet the situation of the story is unquestionably linked to that of the other four, for the child's father was a casualty of the insurrection.

Why the insistence on first-person narrative, with the predominance of the aforementioned dual focus? This uniformity of narrative structure must be considered to be exceptionally important to Roa. In "Slaughter" we saw at least three principal characteristics of this voice. In a suggested ascending order of importance, they are: (1) the relativity of the human grasp of reality—a first-person narrative can be used to show the vicissitudes of the individual perception of events; (2) the fallacy of a romantic and overly emotional commitment, which may be either inherently destructive or at least nonconducive to effective action; (3) an expression of a collective but perhaps fragmentary consciousness. Paradoxically, (1) and (3) are almost the opposite of each other, for the former implies a relativity of individual belief and sentiment, while the latter suggests the crystallization of a collective unconsciousness into the expressive power of one individual. Of course, this expressive power may be manifested in the illusion of deliberate literary creation (the artist) or in the illusion of the unknowing spokesman, whose words we are permitted to overhear or whose preverbalized interior thoughts we are privileged to have access to.

In "Slaughter" an ironic attitude toward the expression of collective sentiment tends to predominate, and, in reality, we might say that the old woman as well as the young narrator are "correct" in their respective versions. In "Bajo el puente" ("Under the Bridge")[11] and in "Cuerpo presente" ("Lying in State")[12] this irony has disappeared, and the same (?) narrator can be considered more properly the embodiment of a popular collective sentiment. Needless to say, he is unaware of this honored role and his narration, now from the point of view of a child speaking, is the artistic illusion of privileged access rather than the story of a conscious raconteur.

In "Under the Bridge" we are presented with the suicide of the old schoolteacher, don Cristaldo. Told from a child's point of view the story is the most difficult of the five and the one with the greatest amount of unexplained motivation and the most expressionistic presentation. Don Cristaldo seems to have represented not a notion of progress for that miserable village lost in the great Chaco, but rather a figure of human dignity and the belief in the value of self-esteem: "We followed his words without understanding. The things he said did not belong to that moment. They happened a long time ago. Or they were yet to happen. He lived in wait. He said, 'One day a stranger is going to arrive here. And you won't see him if you aren't prepared.' Words, like his breath, failed him" (*M*, 28).

Structurally speaking, the interest of the story lies in the difficulty the reader has in finding a point of reference for the narrator's apparently disjointed recollections of the teacher. One realizes that Roa has deliberately chosen a fragmentary and confusing form of presentation to replace the tidy "not A, but B" structure that makes "Slaughter" initially transparent. In "Under the Bridge" the almost surrealistic nature of the narrator's recollection correlates with his own inability to understand the full extent of the old man's words and his actions. Indeed, his suicide appears almost to contradict his alleged "waiting." But even more than our appreciation of the narrator's difficulties of comprehension, we realize how his recollections do coalesce into some sort of pattern. The old man's suicide beneath the bridge among the waterlilies that he planted with his own hands is a gesture of final despair over the dreadful hopelessness of the human condition in a spiritual and geographic wasteland. But this suicide is also a sacrificial gesture that strikes a responsive chord in the villagers and the child-witness. Much later it will also touch the adult narrator, whose voice is, like the schoolteacher's actions, the attempt to "go back to the beginning," to return to the remote cause and to understand it:

And I find that a heap of years have passed since then. I am now as old as the teacher was when he hurt himself under the bridge, that morning when all us students went in file to see his face beneath the muddy waters. All at once he had flown back, back to the beginning. What we saw from the bridge among the smell of the royal water lilies (that now also had the smell of dogs), was the wrinkled face of a child. Less than that: the face of a newborn. The murky water was certainly a bit deceiving. Someone was approaching down the road, swaying from side to side among the reflections. At first we thought it was the [school] inspector and we became a little alarmed. Not knowing what to do, someone started to sing the national anthem, and soon we were all following along. A strong chorus, off-key, as though we were singing at the foot of the flagpole, our eyes turned toward whoever was coming toward us. (*M*, 36)

   With his child-narrators, it is apparent that Roa is able to capture the bewildered but all-encompassing curiosity of the young, as well as a "purer," less romantic, and less cynical point of reference. And, given the ineffectualness of his characters who subscribe to Western rationalism, Roa also probes the profounder perceptions of the untutored, primitive mind: the savage mind of which I have already spoken.[13] In terms of narrative structure the problem is one of preserving this "impressionistic innocence," while at the same time endowing it with the mythic qualities of the spokesman who unknowingly gives voice to the collective unconscious and its search for meaning in experience. The interplay of these two perspectives—one linked to the need to return to the uncontaminated beginning and the other to the artist's goal of providing a coherent representation of his particular vision—is particularly evident in "Lying in State." This is the last of the five pieces and returns to the figure of Chepé Bolíviar. His body, waked by the villagers, "lies in state," and, since the chronological point of reference is the time of his death, the narrator's focus is limited to a much earlier point in time than it is in "Slaughter," where Chepé's reputation in the years after his death is also a concern.

   The presence of Chepé's body lying in state in his laboriously wrought coffin is the central point of reference for the story, and with it comes the inevitable references to the man's ambiguous meaning for the villagers and to the battle that is raging around them between insurrectionists and government forces. Chepé is thus a mute symbol for an especially immutable conjunction of circumstances, the embodiment of an unending cyclical return:[14] "But just imagine, insisting on dying on a night like this. But that's how he always was. He was one of those people who live waiting for what can't happen to happen and there's no doubt he got from the Evangelist that business about there being no death because what went before has already happened. Without even a by-your-leave that man has left us his body like someone who gives away what he can no longer use" (*M*, 43).

This is a curious combination. On the one hand, we have the stony silence of Chepé's body, which is no less a mysterious enigma in death that in the shadowy madness of the last years of his life. On the other hand, there is the almost overly loquacious narrator, whose tone comes close to that of the *comadre*, the neighborhood gossip. This is certainly a deliberate technical ploy on Roa's part, for with it he captures the way in which the narrator-spokesman is intimately linked to Chepé's "presence," almost so much so that the body is simply another piece of furniture to be treated as an inconvenience. Yet he also captures the same narrator's attempt to fit the pieces together and to justify somehow the particular burden of that body's presence: "Of course, none of this has anything to do with what I am saying. The funny thing is that when you want to talk about one thing you always end up talking about another" (*M*, 46). The irony of this assertion as it touches upon literary narrative hardly requires belaboring.

What does emerge through the apparently pertinent observations, supported by the apparently unpertinent ones, is this strange "return to the beginning" that don Cristaldo sought and to which he made reference in the words he carved on the surface of Chepé's coffin. The most immediate "beginning" that comes to mind is that of the Eternal Return, the seeking after the primogenial roots, after the uncorrupted innocence of an earlier human state prior to the spiritual burdens borne by man in his present state. Of paramount importance in appreciating Roa's choice of narrative voice and the structure of dual perspective, the narrator's recollections and his efforts to interpret what he is able to remember are also attempts to "return to the beginning." Not to the beginning of mankind, nor to the beginning of a suffering race or people, but to an individual beginning, to the source of one man's burden of memory and the particular anguish it brings to him. In the end, the only significant difference between the return to the beginning seemingly accomplished by Don Cristaldo, Chepé, and the unnamed narrator is that the latter's is a return via verbal expression given literary form. No claim is made that this is a preferred form of "return" for man. But it is undeniable

that it permits a communication of the event; in the case of the two
older men, the mystery of their own return to the beginning remains
forever inaccessible in the silence imposed both by life and by death.

The rhetoric of Roa's stories is in this sense one of interior
duplication, for the substance of man's return to his beginnings—to
his youth through the human gift of self-contemplating memory—is
precisely the return to their own unnamed beginnings by the
spiritual forebears of his childhood. The ramblings of the narrator in
"Lying in State" give a superficial impression of an inconsequential
and utterly forgettable reality: "But let's forget about all that. It's said
and done with, and I don't want to bore you. Let's get on with what
concerns us" (M, 47). But once again the narrator's words are
(unknowingly?) ironic. If that particular Paraguayan reality ranges, in
a documentary, from what is trivial and boring in provincial life to the
awesome misery of an oppressed people, the intangible mystery of
the quest for the beginning and for "what existed before the
beginning" implies a human experience that is profoundly moving in
its implications. The fact that man possesses these deeply felt needs
to somehow discover his roots and to come to terms with the
overwhelming ambiguity of his existence is one of his most
distinguishing—and mythic—qualities. And that art is metaphoric of
that mythic quest and of the attempt to "explain" that quest is one of
its unquestionable justifications.[15]

Without being able to present a coherent explanation of Chepé's
quest and without appearing to sense the irony of his quest after the
quest, the narrator's ramblings do, however, lead him to an articulation of the sense of fulfillment provided by the quest, which
nevertheless remains for the reader more meaningful in its enigmatic
suggestiveness than in any conclusive interpretation we might give to
it:

We were busy with that when all of a sudden a yellow and blue flash lit up the
side of the hill. Then another and another. The thunder rolled heavily over
the valley. We thought the deluge would return. But then it became the
bursts of the machine guns and the rifle-fire that spilled out everywhere. That
was the morning when the government batteries bombarded the bridge and
split it in two. That same day the loyalists occupied the city. The circus gave
two or three performances for the soldiers and then moved on somewhere
else with its people and its animals. All just like in the beginning and us
wanting it to start all over again. (M, 51–52)

IV *"Juegos nocturnos": The Legitimacy of Humanitarian Sentiment*

The structural complexity of Roa's stories is well demonstrated by "Juegos nocturnos" ("Nocturnal Games"),[16] the title story of a group of pieces set in Buenos Aires, where Roa has lived along with tens of thousand of fellow exiles since 1947. Many of the pieces in this group concern the large Paraguayan exile population in the Argentine capital.[17] "Nocturnal Games" inevitably concerns the same problems to be found in the bulk of Roa's fiction, and there is a strong undercurrent of sarcastic denunciation of a particular closed point of view that refuses or is unable to accept the human situation, particularly as it is experienced by the silent masses, with sympathy and understanding. The manipulation of a complex narrative structure is, as we have alleged, valuable to Roa in an attempt to go beyond explicit political denunciation. In order to utter denunciations, the committed individual does not need literature. But if he believes that art provides a commentary more powerful than "direct pronouncements," the artist must exploit the particular mannerisms of literature. Roa is unquestionably a mannerist, an author whose writing is foregrounded in its studied difficulty. The direct result is a reading experience that is arduous; indirectly the reader must consider carefully the importance of each statement made and avoid the sort of skimming permitted by more transparent forms of literature. The back cover of the collection *Slaughter* repeats a statement by Roa that is symptomatic of a generation of mannerist writers (for whom the literary historian usually sees Borges as the progenitor) and indicative of a belief that radical commitment can be found in man's suprareality and expressed in fictions that capture that elusive level of man's consciousness: "For me reality is what is left when reality has completely disappeared, when the memory of habit has been burned, the forest that prevents us from seeing the tree. We can only refer to it vaguely, or dream it, or imagine it."

"Nocturnal Games" concerns the suprareal level of consciousness of an individual. Although there is a skeleton of an exterior framework that introduces the man in the opening sentence (" 'No,' the man said" [*M*, 55]) and relates his falling heavily asleep at the end of the story, the bulk of the narrative is a stream-of-consciousness recreation of (1) his reactions as he reads a book on poverty by one Harrington (on p. 60 there is the indication that the author is not Argentine and the implication that maybe that it is John Kenneth

Galbraith's *The Affluent Society*); (2) his previous conversations with
some acquaintances, including a Paraguayan poet, on the nature of
poverty; (3) his chance encounter with an English woman living in
Buenos Aires and eternally grieving the death of her husband in a
bombing raid during World War II; (4) his virtually unconscious
overhearing of a brutal lover's quarrel between two youths to whom
he appears to "rent" the inner patio of his house in Olivos.

The man's "inner reality" is strikingly impoverished. It is a mixture
of vague liberal shibboleths, an almost reactionary ignorance concerning the complexities of human society (for example, he maintains
the belief that the present is chaos and that there is a remote,
primeval state that was preferable), the simplistic notion that poverty
is only a question of not having enough to eat, and the quaintly
romantic belief that the stark existence of the poor commends itself
for its lack of complications. The consciousness of Roa's character is, in
short, hardly attractive, and Roa makes use of some standard ploys to
discredit the man. For example, in this passage juxtaposition makes
commentary unnecessary:

He stood there looking at the remains of his dinner, his arms crossed on his
abdomen. For a moment all you can hear is his voice muttering in the dark:
"It's something more subtle, insidious, that our body, its reflexes, the misery
of habit use in order to drag you down. A kind of deaf anger, a moral cramp
that spreads its burning in all directions. . . . Hmmm . . . . Hmmm . . .
that accumulates this bad taste in the mouth." His ball of spit is heard hitting
the tile of the sink and then the sound of water from the faucet. (*M*, 59)

This use of a negatively valued stream of consciousness is particularly effective in that it permits the reader to see in some detail the
train of thought that for another writer, might simply be denounced
in its exterior manifestations. We see instead the insidious reasoning
that is involved, the hypocrisy, the abysmal lack of sensitivity toward
others, the sort of patronizing way of thinking about people that
economic security often brings. Daniel Moyano was able to sustain an
entire novel on this principle, and *El oscuro (The Dark One)* is an
example of the elaboration of a "psychiatric myth" in the sense that
Moyano uses the suprareal, unconscious dimension to portray a
police-state mentality that is the hallmark of certain political systems.[18] In Roa's case, my impression is that what is involved is not the
patronizing superiority of the Argentine petit bourgeois toward the
Paraguayan (usually destitute) exile, but the representation of a

generalizable attitude of the "have" toward the "have-not." Since the have-nots tend to be the common denominator of all known human societies, the assumption is that Roa's unnamed consciousness is universally reprehensible.

The narrative time of the story extends over a brief stretch of the present, during a late hour of the evening in which "el hombre"—the man—is reading Harrington's book, his window open to the sounds of a neighborhood dance; he is also awaiting the arrival of the two lovers, his "clients." It is this segment of the story which makes for difficult reading. His semiconsciousness passes back and forth between the book, his "thoughts" on it and immediately past conversations with acquaintances on poverty and his generous "arrangement" for the two lovers: "Well, let's see if you can find in all of Olivos a place better suited than this one to your needs" (*M*, 55). The last paragraphs constitute a denouement of considerable abruptness—again, a jux-taposition that requires no "outside" commentary—and are in marked contrast to the bulk of the story. We learn, through the man's semiconsciousness, of the arrival of the young man and woman, their quarrel, the woman's brutal mistreatment by the man, and their precipitous withdrawal. Barely aware of what has taken place, the man falls into a heavy sleep with the reading lamp still on. The abruptness with which these events take place serves as a definitive rejection of the man's hypocritical attitude toward the lovers. Al-though we need not summarize in detail his attitudes toward poverty, since they constitute Roa's elaboration of the story itself, we can characterize those attitudes as a sort of romantically ignorant eulogy of what Oscar Lewis called the "culture of poverty."

The latter term is well chosen, for sociologists-anthropologists as well as humanists have concerned themselves with the spiritual and emotional effects of poverty, quite beyond the tangibles of a statistical account of crime rates, infant mortality, infectious diseases, and so on. One thinks, for example, of Lewis's stunningly effective re-portages on the culture of poverty in Mexico (*Five Families, The Children of Sanchez*) and Puerto Rico (*La vida*). These and other works present the culture of poverty in so dramatic a fashion that they can be called examples of documentary or nonfiction narrative. As a consequence, it is difficult for the informed reader to maintain the Heidiesque illusion of a primitive simplicity inherent to the culture of poverty. The Western reader has had at least since naturalism versions of Arcadian peasantry that are less than inviting (for example, in Thomas Hardy's novels), but only more recent urban

perspectives have dealt in any depth with the phenomenon of
poverty in the city. Social realism of the 1930s and 1940s approached
the subject, but almost invariably with the promise of a solution
attendant upon social revolution. For most middle-class readers,
however, such literature often leaves no impression due to its
simplemindedness. For the latter reader there appears to be the
rather unshakeable belief in the promise of liberal institutions to
remedy socioeconomic misfortunes and the quaint but disturbing
notion that the poor somehow have it better because they are
uncontaminated by the complications of middle-class existence. We
might call this the *West-Side Story* syndrome: poverty set to innocu-
ous song and dance, a "cute" and therefore harmless pseudotragedy.
Compare the following two quotes from the man's semiconscious
ramblings:

"But if it's only a question of eating, there's the plankton—is that the word,
you who read *Reader's Digest?* That could be a solution, right? Everybody
back to the sea, to live in the sea, where there's food for everybody. . . ."
(*M*, 57)

"These kids, no. They come in and go back to their corner completely
These two scamps love life, love each other. It's all they've got. They're poor,
but they're rich. And if good fortune exists on earth, they are fortunate. You
have everything, and you're missing half of it. I have my piano, Mozart,
Bach, Beethoven. I've got the house. But for them the shadow cast by the
weeds in the garden is enough. I'm poorer than they are—do you see the
difference?" (*M*, 61).

It is typical of Roa's quiet yet incisive irony that the man falls asleep
without seeming to register on any but the most basic level of
consciousness the events taking place that night out in his inner patio.
The two lovers are far from being pre-Fall figures of Adam and Eve,
blissfully hidden among the Edenic weeds of the simple bower the
man furnishes them. The violent change that takes place between the
man and woman is not reported to us in full, and we are meant to
receive it in the fragmentary fashion in which it filters through the
man, who is on the very edge of oblivious sleep. However from what
we can gather, the woman has angered the man in some way, his
latent frustrations emerge in a rage of jealously, and he insults the
woman with the "palabra infame" ("the infamous word"—that is,
whore). He strikes her brutally, knocking her against the patio wall.
In short, a rather inevitable conclusion for an at best precarious

relationship. The impoverished Adam and Eve stricken, finally, by the Fall, their Edenic bower in the end nothing but a weed-choked inner patio of a dingy suburban house.

Part of the complexity of Roa's story is the juxtapostion between the two segments, the lack of an adequate impression on the mind of "el hombre" and the obligation imposed on the reader to reconsider the details of the former's ramblings in the light of the intense brutality of the lover's quarrel. Needless to say, there is no need for any explicit commentary as far as the author is concerned. A proper comprehension of the structural juxtapostion is enough to enable the reader to see the foolishness and the danger of so ignorant an attitude toward the reality of the poor:

A frightened sound of feet can be heard, the sound of a body that has fallen to its knees getting up, clutching the wall, fleeing clumsily in its own panic, causing the dry rose bushes to rustle as it goes by, stumbling blindly against the rotten wood of the outer door.
  "No," the man said, seated on the bed and rubbing his eyes. "No I don't know," he said as he struggled to remember something. (*M*, 62).

Inevitably, the house assumes almost allegorical proportions. It would be easy, although simplistic, to see the man and his house, part of which he "generously" makes available to the lovers, as a symbol of dominance by the middle class. They are enclosed in the spiritual and material cocoon of their own restricted reality, excluding the masses from power and only making limited concessions of admittance, as does the man to the lovers—for a price of course. Come what may, the enclosed reality remains essentially unaffected, just as the man falls asleep oblivious to the harsh drama that has occurred. To insist on the details of such an allegorical dimension for "Nocturnal Games" would be unimaginative. Yet there is no question that the choice of an "inner" frame of reference for his story, first the house and then the man's ignorant consciousness, provides Roa with the sort of concentrated focus that makes for a very successful short story.

On the other hand, "Contar un cuento" ("To Tell a Story")[19] is perhaps the least satisfactory of Roa's recent stories.[20] An observer's account of a quasi-legendary raconteur's tale of his own death, which occurs as he concludes his story, this piece is perhaps too reminiscent of Borges. Not that Borges has any exclusive claim to this sort of story. But the "wonderment" of the event, in contrast to Roa's other

unremittingly ironic pieces, is almost sentimental, a circumstance
compounded perhaps by the use of a firsthand instead of an omnis-
cient narrator. Yet "To Tell a Story" is Roa's most clearly "metaliterary" story, and we have already quoted (and attributed to Roa himself)
one of the raconteur's opinions, which the publishers print on the
back cover of *Slaughter*. The following assertion is noteworthy for its
implied rejection of documentary art and parallels closely Borges's
own statement about the writer's ultimate discovery that his artifices
are the pattern not of a higher truth, but of the lines of his own face:
"And the life of man? But does anyone know anything about this man
condemned to death other than the scrawls he scratched on the walls
of his cell? And at times those smudges trick us even more because we
infuse them with our own agony and indifference" (*M*, 64).

The unnamed raconteur—"el gordo"—reappears in the story "El y
el otro" ("He and the Other One"),[21] which is superficially distinguished by the total lack of comma and period punctuation, a
procedure surely meant to enhance the unchecked flow of the
storyteller's words and the total suppression of the listener by that
flow. (In terms of narrative context, the "listener," who is the
author-reporter, intervenes only at the very beginning to identify the
speaker: "the fat man said" [*M*, 69].) The tale itself concerns an
ostensibly chance incident between a pickpocket and a well-dressed
man on a crowded Buenos Aires subway train. But it is interpreted by
the teller as an example of "fatal destinies": "these two need a whole
multitude to hide their mystery and to know that they are alone they
need this whole sad smell of catacombs to end up by finding out that
they have been linked together from the beginning . . ." (*M*, 80).

As "proof" of his interpretation of the occurrence, which he claims
to have witnessed, the raconteur weaves together three separate
stories, this one event and two others. All three are meant to support
the hypothesis of "fatal destinies" within the framework of a chaotic
universe: "haven't you realized that everything tends toward confusion and disorder and that perpetual peace and the harmony of the
spheres and all that jazz of the philosophers doesn't really happen
except in your head?" (*M*, 76). Beyond the matter of fatal destinies
there is also the suggestion of a metaliterary concern: the nature of
the material the storyteller deals with. Structurally and as an
example of harmony imposed by the telling of three separate
mysterious events, what we have is what may be called narrative
parataxis,[22] the apparently random (but of course determined)
running together of separate narrative threads.

V *"Borrador de un informe": Outline for Private Infamy*

The most difficult story to understand from within, so to speak, is "Borrador de un informe" ("Draft of a Report"),[23] the lead story in a group of pieces set in Paraguay. As in "Nocturnal Games," "Draft" is characterized by a "negative narrator," a narrative reporter whose summary addressed to higher authorities is a self-betrayal. From the outset we should make clear what the story only reveals clearly at the end: the unnamed interventor, sent to maintain order during the religious celebrations of Kaacupé on December 8 (Feast of the Immaculate Conception) in honor of the national virgin of Paraguay, is, like several of Roa's male characters in *Thunder Among the Leaves*, a weak and destructive figure. The interventor represents on a public level the all-powerful forces of the repressive state. On a personal level, he is a man haunted (apparently) by epilepsy and (unquestionably) by a sexual impotence that has become a self-hating obsession. The two levels merge (as psychoanalytic biography has shown for more than one public figure, with Hitler being the archetype) when the interventor's own personal problems become the source of public disruption in the events surrounding the religious festival.

The narrative substance of the story is relayed via two mediums. First, we have the interventor's summary proper, which if read on its own is sketchy and unrevealing of the nature of the events. Superficially, it is a typical bureaucratic document that fulfills the demand for its existence without really being informative. Intercalated throughout the summary are nine parenthetical asides representing the interior monologue of the interventor as his innermost thoughts interrupt his composition of the summary. Naturally it is by means of these interruptions that we discover the true explanation of what happened, the chicanery of the interventor with regard to the fabulous sums of money collected by the church as donations to the Virgin of Kaacupé and, finally, his personal infamy toward the Mary Magdalene prostitute that figures prominently in the religious festivities.

By using an unreliable public narrator who silently interrupts himself to reveal reliably (to betray, really), his true character, Roa achieves a tripartite perspective: that of the people, that of officialdom, and that of a particularly despicable servant of the latter whose personal weaknesses are an instrument of a betrayal of the former. As a public servant, someone sent to intervene in the name of the national authorities and to insure that the fabulous donations to the

Virgin pass into the hands of civil rather than church authorities, the
official adopts a condescending attitude toward the people. In his
eyes and in the words that he uses in his summary to his chiefs, the
people are a sorry and fanatic lot of whom the major religious feast
signifies more an opportunity for revelry and commercial gain than
respect toward a national symbol: "From the window of the court-
house I have seen them coming down the hill along the highway that
the Americans are building. Interminable lines, just like ants, with
their possessions on their backs, which from a distance seems to be the
visible bundles of their faith, the humps of their needs. It's not like we
deny them their rights, such as this one of having hope in the grace of
God" (M, 45).

The mixture of official patronizing and a point of view that sees
peasant pilgrims as hoards of ants invading the North American's
highway (a symbol of official pride) places the narrator on a level of
disdain for a phenomenon he can only barely grasp. When he goes on
with his patronizing gestures toward the pilgrims, recognizing that
"peasants will be peasants," he unconsciously ironizes his own point
of view: "You ask yourself how they allow [these traveling salesmen]
to enter the Miracle Worker's town. And it must be because in life
everything is all mixed together: the good and what is a little dirty,
the holy and what is a little bit the devil's" (M, 87).

Although we sense that the interventor writes these words pat-
ronizingly, they are ironically representative of a human meaning
that lies really beyond his grasp. One thinks of the Spanish phrase, "la
gran feria del mundo" (the great world's fair), a phrase metaphoric of
human nature and of human society, of how sin and grace are
intimately intertwined. Nowhere is this more obvious in the story
than in the Mary Magdalene figure, the prostitute who pays for her
sins in advance by making the pilgrimage to the shrine bearing a
life-size and heavy cross. Once in the village and confident of the
Virgin's protection, she puts up her temporary boudoir and makes
her body available to the weary male pilgrims. This mixture of sin and
grace, of retribution and profit, is officially incomprehensible. Yet it
is important within the structure of the story as an indication of a
complex and fluid human circumstance that lies beyond the understanding of simpleminded, officious rigidities:

I was about to say something, but the words stuck in my throat, for at that
moment in the gap in the tent she appeared—the penitent that had arrived
with the cross on her back and the mystic aureola of one who has been

illuminated! Someone must have whispered to her that the delegation car was in front of her, a car in which I sat, unable to come out of my stupor. But it didn't seem to matter much to her and she only made a mocking face and then went back in, never stopping fanning herself. Imagine, Coronel, my indignation! (*M*, 98)

The preceding quote serves a double purpose, as do most of the passages in the official summary. On the one hand, we can appreciate the hypocrisy of the public statement, the unctuous tone of the interjection and the false indignation that it communicates (in one of the asides the intervenor notes to himself that such statements are important in the event that his report reaches the newspapers; see *M*, 93). On the other hand, from the retrospective point of view established by the closing pages of the text, we perceive a foreshadowing of the unreported relationship between the intervenor and the prostitute and of the uncontrollable epilepsy triggered by his sexual excitement. Both the man's epilepsy and his sexual deficiencies can be seen as an overly facile device on Roa's part, like the uncontrollable and self-destructive kleptomania of the "good" civil servant in "Private Audience." In both cases a weakness that in reality lies beyond human control (and therefore one for which the individual cannot justifiably be held accountable) is made to symbolize a personality defect. But this criticism aside, the corruption of the minor official, the willing servant of an even more corrupt higher power, is acceptably represented by a range of emotional weaknesses symbolized by epilepsy and sexual impotence, both of which are presented as destructive infirmities which corrode from within: "I can feel my mouth filling again with this bitter and hot taste, like something that has been burned, the jolt of an anxiety that again grows, that I spit out around me like bits of my own poison" (*M*, 102; this last passage is part of the last aside).

Within the structure of the story—the dual point of view—the intervenor's psychological sickness touches upon two events of the people's religious festivities, one expressed in public terms (it relates to the intervenor's official duties and is duly described in the report) and one expressed in private terms (and consequently only given adequate clarification in an aside not recorded in the report). As we are able to tell by implication from the summary and more explicitly from the first aside, the intervenor's primary assignment is not to insure public order during the religious festivities or to protect the pilgrims from the guerrillas hiding in the mountains. Rather, it is to take possession in the name of the government, for "safekeeping," of the donation boxes and their considerable contents. The penultimate sentence of the summary reports the transmittal of 132 urns and seven large boxes of donations, a considerable amount considering the extreme poverty among the Paraguayan peasantry. As the parish priest is reported to have said, no one had ever attempted to rob the church of the donations, and in the past they had always been destined without disturbance for the activities of the church. In order to comply with his orders, the interventor arranges the confiscation of the donations with the aid of the judge and the chief of police, who pretend to rob the church office to demonstrate the need for official custodianship. When they are surprised in their entrance into the church disguised as bandits, the priest shoots them. With no remaining witness to his intentions, the interventor takes the donations into his safekeeping and the priest, an unwitting accomplice in a beautifully successful operation, is sent to the capital for reassignment. The interventor's public attitude is the sort of cynicism associated with official operations based on deceit and betrayal, where personal designs of those in power are translated by force and by rhetoric into an illusion of public good. One has the impression in the end, however, that the priest suspects that something has been left untold:

The priest has been by to say good-bye. When he saw the stack of urns that are in safekeeping in the office, he murmured sadly: "A whole harvest lost!" I thought he was referring to the lamentable end to one of the most brilliant functions in many years and to its moral consequences. In these terms, I answered him with the saying: "The good seed bears fruit after the storm and feeds the most needy." (The meaning of what he said with respect to the "seed" locked in the urns, although sybilline, was clear enough. But what did he mean when, looking down and seeing the little puddles of my saliva by the table, he added, "Don't water it too much, for you can ruin it.") (*M*, 97; the parenthetical passage is the first part of the seventh aside.)

The priest is obviously referring, in the first statement reported, to the loss of funds for the church, which is made obvious by the interventor's aside. The latter's cynical use of a pious biblical saying is answered by the priest's almost sarcastic reference to the former's epilectic spittal. We assume the priest means that the official should be careful not to overdo things in his self-satisfied cleverness; that the interventor does not get the meaning of the comment hardly requires belaboring. With reference to the "proper" destiny for the donations of the faithful, the words of the priest make it clear that pieties are not involved, but rather to whom will befall the booty of the faithful's devotion to the Virgin of Kaacupé. Roa does not imply that the church is justified in its claims on the donations. More important, we sense, are the wishes of the people. In another context, their attachment to the Virgin might be a lamentable enslavement to a religious myth. But in this more immediate context, in despoiling the church of the contributions and in transmitting them to the civil authorities for the latter's personal gain, the official is party to a cynical charade that deprives the people of one of their most elemental rights, the right to honor their gods in their own way and with the money they have earned with their own blood. Retrospectively, the early sentence, "It's not like we deny them their rights, such as this one of having hope in the grace of God" (*M*, 85), becomes a token of the authorities' ugly cynicism toward the people.

On the personal level, the interventor, after several meetings with the prostitute that he does not report to his "Señor Coronel," arranges her murder with a venomous snake. This is to punish her and to avenge him for her mocking discovery of his sexual impotence. The event is reported as a circumstantial accident, as are the deaths of the police chief and the judge, and, as far as the people are concerned, they are left to understand the death of the notorious woman as they will. The cynicism in this context arises from the official's hypocrisy toward the prostitute's public exercise of her profession and his taking her for his own use and his subsequent psychopathic murder of her because of his own limitations as a man. In short, where on one level the people as a whole have been betrayed by the official, on another level one representative figure of that "gran feria del mundo" has been betrayed as yet another manifestation of the sick mentality embodied in the paragon of authority. As a memento of the woman, he keeps her watch after her death: "(Every night I wind that cheap, miserable watch, which ticks weakly inside the case corroded by the salt of her wrist, which ticked deafeningly next to my ear when, kneeling in front of her, she held my head with her hands, laughing, making fun of me, of my secret. But despite her scorn, which was perhaps her way of loving and of understanding, no one has ever understood that secret as profoundly as she did. That's why she's dead)" (*M*, 101).

The prostitute pays with her life for the discovery of the man's synecdochal secret, a secret that is a personal problem symbolic of a personality pattern. It is only in these terms that we can reconcile the several perplexing aspects of the story, like the choice of the official document plus the asides as the narrative vehicle, the context of a popular religious festival of enormous significance to the collective masses, the interplay of a cynical act of public betrayal and an act of private destruction. It is clear that the two acts are to be seen as the general and the particular manifestations of a singular human attitude, an attitude cleverly reflected in the pomposity of the official summary, in what we can read between the lines and in what we learn and abstract from the asides. The particular ugliness of that attitude is emphasized by the supposedly virtuous context of the religious feast, but which is in reality only a particularly valuable opportunity to defraud the populace. Given this sort of careful artistic pattern, Roa Basto hardly need resort to heated rhetoric of denunciation in order to impress the reader with the nature of the circumstance being described. The closing statement of the summary is appropriately ironical. Although overtly addressed to his superior by the intervenor, it may be taken equally as an apostrophe to the reader by the author: "I hope that this rather jumpy report gives you more or less an approximate idea of the things that have taken place, and I take this opportunity to repeat to you that I am your loyal servant and friend" (*M*, 102).

VI *Conclusions*

Although I have examined in some detail only four of the approximately twenty stories Roa has published since *Thunder Among the Leaves*, these stories (and the half-dozen other referred to more summarily) are indicative of the orientations of his current production. These stories are characterized by the attempt to make the sense of "commitment" more subtle and to envelope the story in a narrative form that affirms its autonomy as literary expression while becoming at the same time an integral part of the way in which we understand that tale. All literary structure is a form of commentary on what it is conveying. But modern fiction has sought a complexity and a variety of structurings that, far more than "traditional storytelling" can match the complex nature of our contemporary perceptions of reality. Roa's recent stories, particularly the ones examined in this chapter, are excellent examples of that search.

CHAPTER 5

Yo el Supremo: *The Curse of Writing*

I *Introduction*

THE year 1974 saw the publication of novels by three of the foremost figures of the Latin American new novel. Despite the publication of short stories and/or essays, none had contributed a major work in over a dozen years to a rapidly evolving literary phenomenon, and thus the appearance of their works was an important literary event. Cuba's Alejo Carpentier published *El recurso del método (The Recourse of the Method)*, Argentina's Ernesto Sabato (now writing his last name without the accent mark over the first vowel) published *Abaddón el exterminador (Abaddón the Exterminator)*, a novel many had come to believe was never to appear, and Paraguay's Augusto Roa Bastos published *Yo el Supremo (I, the Supreme)*,[1] a work that had been "finished" several times, but that the author insisted on polishing and repolishing with his own laborious craftsmanship.

All three novels received an initially favorable critical reception, and it is difficult to predict which of the three will emerge as the most significant: all are excellent works from the pens of mature writers. But more than just the casual link of their publications in 1974 after their authors' lengthy novelistic parenthesis binds these novels together. It appears that all are related to a casual agreement reached a dozen years ago between a group of Latin American novelists that each would devote a novel to the figure of a major dictator of his own country.[2] José Lezama Lima's *Paradiso* is set against the backgrop of the Machado dictatorship in Cuba, while Mario Vargas Llosa's *Conversación en La Catedral (Conversation in The Cathedral)* evokes the moral putrefaction of the Odría regime in Perú. Guillermo Cabrera Infante's *Tres Tristes Tigres (Three Trapped Tigers)* is an apocalyptic vision of the waning days of the Batista government in

91

Cuba. The three novels published in 1974 also concern dictators or periods of infamous dictatorship. Unlike the others, Carpentier's novel is not based on a historical figure, but is rather a highly imaginative composite of that abiding Latin American phenomenon. Sabato's novel covers the last days of the 1966–1973 series of disastrous military leaders in Argentina. Finally Gabriel García Márquez published in 1975 his long awaited *El otoño del patriarca* *(The Autumn of the Patriarch)*, which also deals with a composite dictator.

If Carpentier's and García Márquez's novels depart from the others in evoking a composite figure, Roa's is unique in reaching back to the nineteenth century. While the dictatorships associated with the early decades of Latin American independence from Spain provide a rich panorama of individuals and events—one thinks immediately of Argentina's Rosas, who has not been treated adequately in a novel since José Mármol's *Amalia* (1851–1855)—the bulk of the works mentioned deal with figures from recent history. *I, the Supreme*, on the other hand, focuses on the person of one of Latin America's most curious political figures: Dr. José Gaspar Rodríguez de Francia, the mysterious, highly learned man of the French Enlightenment who converted South America's first republic to gain independence from Spain into the first absolute dictatorship on the continent.

The specter of Francia, who claimed to be motivated by the highest principles of political idealism and a desire to preserve the simple innocence of his people, has dominated subsequent Paraguayan history. In fact, an appendix to Roa's novel reproduces documents relating to the ill-fated attempt in 1961 to ascertain the true remains of the Supreme Dictator and to honor them as part of the national patrimony. Yet even this gesture was surrounded by all of the century-old debate over the man's true motives and the uncertainties associated with any aspect of his person, spiritual or physical. It is not necessary to summarize here either the highpoints of Francia's reign (1814–1840) or the intense controversy it has aroused among professional historians and members of the intellectual and power establishments. Suffice it to say, however, that much of Roa's novel is documentary, although it is impossible to say where documentary materials leave off and fiction begins. Unlike other novels on Latin American dictators, which are often content to re-create the sense of an oppressive regime (Odría, for example, does not even appear as a character in Vargar Llosa's two-volume novel), Roa's work is based exclusively on the many voices of Francia himself: Francia speaks of himself, of his government, and of the men and events of his day. The novel, in short, is fictional autobiography, albeit of a highly complex and experimental nature.

II *Image of a Dictator*

It is difficult to know where to begin a characterization of *I, the Supreme*.[3] In the first place, the novel is essentially static: there is no narrative trajectory of events to speak of, no cause-and-effect movement from one incident to another through a set period of time. Of course there is narrative "subject": Francia's own controlling self-image and the text or sequence of interrelated texts that image gives rise to. But recalled historical incident aside, there is no commonplace action. Only 467 pages of text, 456 of which are the mental ramblings of a dying (or dead) man, crazed by the burden of accumulated self-knowledge resulting from a lifetime of intense, unrelenting introspection.

Perhaps it would be best to begin with the tangible aspects of the self-image that Francia projects. We should however note first a standard historical description of Francia, against which the image of the novel may be set. Hubert Herring, in one of the major works on Latin American history, provides a profile of three dictators from the postindependence period. His description of Francia corresponds to the generally accepted historical image of the man:

Austere, frugal, honest, and cruel beyond description, Francia thought only of service to his nation. He hated foreigners bitterly and was fearful of all entanglements. After a few attempts to encourage trade with England, he fell back upon the complete isolation of the nation, forbidding all river traffic to Buenos Aires and permitting few to leave or enter the country. In violent anticlericalism, he broke off relations with the Vatican and appointed his own bishops and clergy. Spaniards, owners of the best lands and businesses, were jailed, murdered, or exiled. Paraguay became a hermit nation, with El Supremo the unchallenged authority. In domestic matters, Francia imposed order, preached the gospel of hard work, and introduced improved methods in agriculture and stock raising. Under his rod, Paraguayans worked tirelessly, making the soil produce more than it ever had before. Critics guilty of a word or gesture against him were jailed, tortured, or murdered. Lacking freedom, Paraguay at least had bread and order. Peace, denied both Argentina and Uruguay during those stormy decades, was assured to Paraguay. Dr. Francia, seventy-four in 1840, could congratulate himself and his people upon their security.[4]

Roa's novel is neither documentary nor historical, although it does attempt to provide some illusion of the former. But unlike antiquarian historical novels, which are customarily characterized by the "thesis" concerning the men and events they recreate, *I, the Supreme* is neither a condemnation nor a revindication of Francia. Nor is it an objective novel, at least not in the sense of scholarly neutrality. The author bases himself first of all on the well-known fact that, in addition to the usual accumulation of documents left by a government, Francia was wont to express his preoccupations in a series of personal diaries. By beginning with this fact, Roa is able to combine fragments of personal and official documents in order to give the illusion of a novel forged wholly from Francia's authenticated self-expression. In addition, the novel includes footnotes containing material taken from contemporary reports, letters, and histories, as well as observations on the main body of the text. Thus, footnotes aside, what the reader confronts are over four-hundred pages of first-person narration.

This narration assumes many forms. Large segments are statements dictated by Francia to his personal secretary, Policarpo Patiño, interrupted by asides to the latter, observations of the latter, and rectifications made by Francia. These segments dominate the novel and present many difficulties because of their only partially differentiated levels. We have on one level the words of Francia engaged in the process of dictating a text (a letter, a proclamation, a memorandum, a personal reminiscence), to which are appended the words of Francia and Patiño as they discuss aspects of the text being dictated; this discussion often takes the form of Francia's abruptly correcting or contradicting himself or fulminating against Patiño for the stupidity of his servile comments. Set against this level involving the act of dictation, composed of the sublevel of the dictated text and that of the asides on the text, we have the level of any one complete segment of the novel, which functions in conjunction with other surrounding segments plus any appended footnotes. In the case of the former level, there is a disjunction between Francia's "real" dictation and the parallel discussion; in the case of the latter there is a conjunction of elements within the segment to produce one total block of text in a work of novelistic fiction. This may seem to many readers like a trivial critical distinction. Yet the reader is faced with what is unquestionably a dense and difficult novel because of the complexity of narrative structure: the reader often has the feeling that he simply does not know what is going on or what the material he is reading has to do with its surrounding context. The nature of the texts purportedly dictated by Francia—texts we presumably witness in the process of being dictated—are a function of the novel's overall complexity.

In addition to the texts dictated by Francia to his secretary (and it should be noted that the reader is often unaware at first that what he has before him is one of these segments), the novel is also composed of selections taken from Francia's *Cuaderno Privado* ("Private Notebook") as well as segments that read as though they were privileged transcriptions of Francia's stream of consciousness. This is what they in fact are in content, although the author is usually careful to provide some indication that these segments are actually further scribblings by the dictator. For example, toward the end of the novel there is a long dialogue between Francia and his dog, Sultán. At first one believes that the novel relays to us verbatim this "conversation." Nevertheless, the conversation in fact concerns Francia's mania for accumulating his own written texts. Sultán, as an example of this mania, sarcastically throws in Francia's face the fact that the latter is engaged in the process of transcribing the argument at the same time that it is taking place. To be sure, from the perspective of the text as one more segment of the novel, it is easy to attribute the dialogue to the fertile imagination of the dictator. This would only serve to reaffirm his mania for producing texts—texts that have a legitimate administrative function (his proclamations, official decisions) or a legitimate autobiographical function (his memoirs concerning the nature of his government and the vicissitudes of his foreign policy) as well as texts that are "fictional" in their creation of nonexistent events and in their transcription of what are plainly the ravings of a paranoid. All of which brings us back to the self-image which Francia projects, willingly or inadvertently, through the novel's illusion of documentary transcription.

The most obvious function of Francia's verbomania, at least in terms of Francia himself, is that of self-justification. Over and over again, Francia explains his actions, decisions, positions. And over and over again he attempts to show how, given the circumstances of the moment, they represented the only viable behavior for a leader charged with the destiny of a country and its people. These passages of self-analysis are unquestionably fascinating and could easily be used as the basis for a sociological interpretation of the novel. Their preponderance may well lead many readers to the superficial conclusion that Roa has written an exoneration of Francia, a revindication of his place in Paraguayan history. Certainly, there are many issues evoked by Francia that run parallel to matters of importance to Latin

America today. And many of the attitudes expressed by Francia jibe with what today is loosely defined as "third-world consciousness": the insistence on the well-being of all of the populace through its identification with a national destiny and the accumulated wisdom of a popular tradition, the debunking of the twin myths of bourgeois progress and capitalism as the only sources of material and therefore spiritual fulfillment, a mistrust of democratic government as a wolf in sheep's clothing (it only masks the rule of a power elite), the dislike and eventually the hatred of self-serving foreign governments that come bearing false promises of assistance, the faith in a dictatorship erected not on the foundations of personal gain (Francia was, as Herring notes, strikingly austere in his personal life) but on a mystical understanding of an intuited will of the people. All of these concerns of Francia are recurring themes in contemporary Latin American political thought.

One of the novel's most striking features needs to be given special mention at this point. While the reader's general impression is that Francia's words are either contemporary to the events he is describing or are recollections of past circumstances, on a number of occasions evidence is presented that Francia is speaking, first, from the perspective of death (Francia is the process of dying and Francia long-since dead) and, second, from the perspective of current events in Latin America. For instance, his comments to Patiño frequently refer to late nineteenth- or twentieth-century occurrences, as for example when he refers to what a pity it is that a dolt like Patiño is the forebearer of one of Paraguay's greatest generals (*Y*, 124; the reference is to Marshal José Félix Estigarribia, the hero of the Chaco War with Bolivia in the 1930s). There is a passing reference to the Brazilian writer, João Guimarães Rosa (*Y*, 132; even Francia's temporal perspective reveals the fact that his is writing from the point of view of a dead man who has access to twentieth-century events: "An author of our own times . . ."). There is a casual reference to the advantages of electric torture ("even though the *picana* might have to be used a little"; *Y*, 94) and there is a clever series of references to a future Paraguayan writer that the knowledgeable reader can only identify as Roa Bastos himself (see *Y*, 102; Francia is discussing his godson, Macario, who appears in the first chapter of Roa's *Son of Man* as the decrepit bearer of the voice of the collective unconscious of the Paraguayan people).

Once we recognize the double perspective of Francia's voice, now speaking in the second quarter of the nineteenth century, now speaking in the last quarter of the twentieth century, we can appreciate how his attempts at self-justification concern both the validity of his political opinions during his tenure as president of Paraguay and their validity in terms of the problems of Latin America today. The epithet "Perpetual Dictator" takes on an unmistakably ironic connotation: his pronouncements are perpetual vis-à-vis his presidency for life and also vis-à-vis their eternal, universal validity for a crisis-ridden Latin America today; thus, many of his pronouncements are titled *Circular Perpetuo* ("Perpetual Circular").

In this same context, the novel's appendix concerning the lost remains of Francia and the debate over contending sets of remains takes on an added significance. Francia speaks throughout the novel not as though he were simply a controversial figure from the remote historical past, but as an individual whose shadow is cast "perpetually" over the destiny of his country. A historian might say that Francia left an indelible stamp on the history of his country and that all subsequent events must be understood in terms of the postindependence Paraguay he created. And this is essentially the implication of Francia's voice (alternately, and on a different level, it is the implication of Roa's novel): that the destiny of Paraguay has been the amalgam of the combined pursuit and abandonment by subsequent leaders of primogenial policies that in Francia's view were the fruit of a profound comprehension of his own people. To this extent, Francia is not a set of decayed remains entombed in a lavish official monument. The disappearance of his physical remains and the fact that all attempts to recover them have failed are correlatives of the extent to how he is, though the novel, the Perpetual Dictator of a lonely, forgotten Paraguay.

In addition to Francia's attempts at self-justification, there are lengthy self-examinations that, as in the case of the dialogue with Sultán the dog, become self-denunciations. It cannot be stressed too much that Roa's novel is not a defense of Francia, but rather a creation of Francia's voice. As he speaks, Francia, in the nature of all men, sees himself obliged to make a defense against his real or imagined detractors. Yet on more than one occasion, in the intense privacy of his own inner person, Francia—the man who rarely sought out contact with other men, the man who, in the midst of a primitive society that he believed to be the preserve of Rousseauistic primitive savages pursued the intellectual concerns of a son of the French Enlightenment—comes face to face with the realization of his own inadequacies, his failures at government, the vanity of his so ardently defended illusions. This man who accords such short shrift to the weaknesses of mankind in general (this is one of the bases of his rejection of liberal democratic institutions), is just as ruthless with himself, even though he may have to objectify his self-condemnation in the voice of an impertinent dog. Francia's intellectual restlessness alternates with his disdain for large portions of human nature, his sense of severe but righteous justice with often appalling intellectual solipsisms, his perceptive disquisitions on the nature of government with vituperative attacks on individuals who he claims have wronged him, his sense of the importance of his role in the history of a continent with his sense of an overwhelming personal isolation.

It would be easy to continue to elaborate on the nature of the self-image that Francia projects throughout this demanding novel; the foregoing comments are only the preliminaries of an adequate characterization of the shadow behind the voice that Roa's work allows to speak at such length and, on so many occasions, so bewilderingly. From the point of view of novelistic structure, Roa's work provides the opportunity for the voice to speak, but an assessment of the nature of that "speaking" reveals that the novel, in accord with a major tenet of contemporary literature, does not presume to decide for us the validity of Francia's Supreme Dictatorship. The rhetoric of the novel attributes the vicissitudes, the contradictions, the excesses of the text or of the documents upon which it draws. It is nevertheless unquestionable that the texture created—a texture in no way any less novelistic for its real and/or alleged documentary inspiration—contributes to the illusion of a neutrality toward the figure of Francia that *I, the Supreme* attempts to maintain:

My opinion is . . . *(the edge of the folio has been burned away)*. . . . In the matter of things opinable all opinions are worse. . . .

But this is not what I wanted to say. Clouds form thick over my head. . . [my ellipsis].

The forms disappear, the words remain, in order to signify the impossible. There is no such thing as a story that can be told. No story that is worth the trouble to be told. But true language has yet to be born. Animals communicate among themselves, without words, better than we, who are proud at having invented them out of the *materia prima* of the chimerical. Without any basis whatever. Without any relation to life . . . [my ellipsis]. (*Y*, 15; ellipses in text.)

III   *History versus Novel*

One superficial conclusion to be drawn from a reading of *I, the Supreme* is that, in the tradition of historical novels, it is based too heavily on documents, that, despite the difficulties it presents to the reader and despite the author's careful choice of material in order to re-create the most complex portrait of Francia possible, what one reads after all are historical documents.[5] The abundance of footnotes substantiates this impression. There are footnotes that are taken from bibliographically identifiable contemporary sources and there are footnotes that are commentaries on the main body of the text. The latter are signed " 'N. del C.'—Nota del Compilador" ("Compiler's Note"). Thus Roa chooses to reinforce the documentary illusion of his work by identifying his role as that not of an author, but of the editor of a critical text. Although perhaps responsible for certain "adjustments" in the text (corrections of obvious errata, addition of "lost" materials, suppression of apocrypha, etc.), he nevertheless presents the text in its most useful scholarly format and clarifies any problems that it may present. Roa does not announce his role in a prologue; rather we surmise it from the notes. However in an italicized colophon in a "Final Note of the Compiler"—he does state explicitly the position we are meant to accept vis-à-vis the text that he has presented:

This compilation has been distilled . . . from some twenty-thousand legal papers, both published and unpublished; from the same number of volumes, pamphlets, periodicals, letters and all manner of secret testimonies that have been consulted, gleaned spied upon, in libraries and archives, both private and official. To this should be added the versions gathered from oral sources and some fifteen-thousand hours of tape recorded interviews, plagued by imprecisions and confusions, with supposed descendents of supposed civil servants, with supposed relatives and "counter"-relatives of the Supreme, who always boasted of having no relatives, and with epigones, panegyrists and detractors who can be called no less supposed and nebulous.

The reader will already have discovered that, opposite from usual texts, this one has been read first and then written. Instead of saying or writing something new, it does no more than copy faithfully what has already been said and composed by others. Therefore, the compilation does not contain a single page, a single sentence, a single word, from the title to this final note, that was not already written in this fashion. "All history which is not contemporary is suspect," the Supreme liked to say. "It is unnecessary to

know how they came to be to know that these fictitious histories do not belong
to the time in which they were written. There is quite a bit of difference
between a book that a private party writes and offers to the public and a book
written by the people. Therefore there can be no doubting that this book is as
old as the people which have dictated it."

Thus, imitating the Dictator once again (dictators fulfill, in fact, this
function: they replace writers, historians, artists, thinkers, etc.), the compiler
declares, in the words of a contemporary author, that the story contained in
these Notes *boils down to the fact that the story that it ought to narrate has*
not been narrated. As a result, the persons and facts that appear in those
notes have earned, by virtue of the ill-fated nature of language, the right to a
fictitious and autonomous existence in the service of the no less fictitious and
anonymous reader. (Y, 467; this passage contains several puns and no attempt
has been made to render them with English equivalents.)

What is to be made of this statement? In the first place, it is obvious
that the text the reader had read up to the point of Roa's statement
cannot be the verbatim transcript of Francia's documents. There is
the matter of the dual level of dictation to which we have already
referred: it is one thing to claim to be reproducing dictated documents. Yet it is quite another to pretend to be reproducing the
conversation between dictator and secretary at the time of dictation,
or that that conversation forms part of the written record (that is, that
Patiño, like a self-starting recording machine, literally recorded
everything that was said in his presence, including by himself). Then
there is also the matter of the verbal style of the texts. Style is being
used here in its general sense, for what we have is an outstanding
example of the "anti-style" of the contemporary novel, the self-
mocking and self-annihilating *écriture* that Roland Barthes and others
have promulgated. So, once again, why this illusion?

There are two possible ways to answer the question. One is to point
to contemporary attitudes toward historical documents, attitudes
reflected by Francia himself in his own texts. Contrary to the
positivistic belief in the ultimately objective value of documents
contemporary to the events they report, we now realize how easy it is
to demonstrate the falsity, the duplicity contained in documentary
sources. Like all of man's writings they too are in the end fictions:
futile attempts to record in the guise of fact that elusive nature of
human circumstances. Modern historians have long known that such
materials must be used with extreme care and that they must be
patiently evaluated before any real value can be assigned to them.
But from a novelist's point of view, their "feignings" (feign is, after all,

the verb from which the noun fiction is derived) make them in the final analysis as "literary" as an overtly novelistic creation. It is this interpenetration between overt fiction and presumed factual sources that has given rise to contemporary documentary literature. In a sense it is the reverse image of the nineteenth-century historical novel. The latter sought to create the illusion of the novel as history; the former shows how the documentary is homologous with fiction. The following "Compilers Note," which identifies for the reader Francia's "Private Notebook" from which many segments of the novel are purportedly taken, describes the unmistakably novelistic nature of its writings in the same terms that have been frequently applied to the Latin American new novel:

Francia's "Private Notebook" is an account book of an unusually large size, like those used by the Supreme from the beginning of his government to put down in his own handwriting, to the last *real*, the accounts of his treasury. In the archives were found more than a hundred of these ledgers of a thousand leaves each. In the last of them, which had barely begun to be used for entering real accounts, there were to be found other entries that were fictitious and cryptic. Only much later was it discovered that, toward the end of his life, the Supreme One had used these pages to put down, unconnectedly and incoherently, facts, ideas, reflexions, insignificant, and almost eccentric observations concerning the most varied of topics and subjects. The ones that seemed to him positive went into the credit column; the negative ones, into the debit column. In this way words, sentences, paragraphs, fragments were duplicated, run on, repeated, or turned around in both columns in the attempt to establish an imaginary balance. They remind one, to a certain extent, of the notations for a polyphonic musical score. It is well known that the Supreme One was a good musician, at least an excellent *vihuela* player, and that he fancied himself a composer.

The fire [referred to in the "Notebooks"] originated in his personal chambers, a few days before his death, and destroyed the account book in large part, along with other legal papers and documents that he was used to keep securely locked away in chests. (Y, 22–23)

An alternate explanation for the question of history versus novel is to extend traditional conventions of the novel. The novel has always pretended to have privileged information concerning characters and events. In the case of the former, the information takes the form of access to diaries, letters, soliloquies, dialogues among characters, and interior monologues, steam of consciousness, not to mention conventions such as speaking from death (Juan Rulfo's *Pedro Páramo* and Roa's own novel), role-switching (Julio Cortázar's *Hopscotch* and

Severo Sarduy's *Cuba with a Song*), "identity annihilation" (José Donoso's *The Obscene Bird of Night* and Carlos Fuentes's *Change of Skin*). The novel by convention takes the reader where he cannot be and is a witness on behalf of the reader; as such, the narrative pretends to more than is "really" possible. (Of course, we might also note conventions in the modern novel of apparent verisimilitude, where every attempt is made to create the illusion that the information is, in fact, not privileged: first-person narratives, "found" texts, internal reporters, etc.)[6]

In the case of Roa's novel, the convention of privileged information is applied to the process of their transcription and compilation rather than to the documents themselves. *I, the Supreme* would be quite another novel if it were simply to reproduce verbatim Francia's proclamations, notebooks, and such and do without the instances of interior duplication whereby the texts purportedly produced by Francia are shuffled together with other texts concerning the production of the former. Only the former can have any claim to documentary authenticity. Therefore, the issue of the extent to which Roa rewrites materials he actually uses from Francia's (or Patiño's) own pen—and there can be, as we have insisted, no question that little if anything attributable directly to the Perpetual Dictator is reproduced verbatim—is in reality of only marginal interest in the discussion of the novel. Those reviewers who may question the validity of *I, the Supreme* as an example of documentary fiction seriously misgauge its nature. What is of central interest is the production of a text, the production of an "inner" text by Francia, either by his own pen or through the medium of dictation to his secretary, and the production of an "outer" text, the novelistic framework that presents Francia in the process of satisfying his verbomania.

The reader may have guessed by now that one of the principal correlatives in the novel is the pun on "dictate" and "dictator." Both derive from the past participle *dictus*, from Latin *dicere*, "to say." The dictator rules by virtue of the fact that what he "says" carries automatically the force of law. In the novel Francia is aware of the etymological relationship between the word that describes his compulsion for creating texts. On one occasion he notes that he is not recording history, but making it. He makes history in the sense that his rule is uniquely influential upon the course of human events and in the sense that his documents "create" history to the extent that they are one (intrinsically fallacious) version of it: "I am not writing history, I am making it. I can remake it according to my will, adjusting, reinforcing, enriching its sense and truth" (*Y*, 210–11). He speaks continually of the need to overcome chance, to impose an order on events—that is, to "write," to "pre-*dict*" history rather than simply experience events passively (see *Y*, 344–45 and 111 passim). For a Napoleonic figure "dictating" history in the sense of controlling events becomes a form of self-affirmation. For Francia the events in which he participated and which he may or may not have controlled in accord with his will are past. Writing from the perspective of, alternately, his dying days and death itself, all that is left for him is to "dictate" history as a form of verbomania that confirms one's existence:

At first I didn't write; I only dictated. Then I would forget what I had dictated. Now I must dictate/write; annotate it somewhere. That's the only way I have of proving that I still exist. Although to be buried in letters, isn't that perhaps the most thorough way to die? No? Yes? So then? No. Emphatically no. The emaciated will of senility. The old life oozes an old man's thoughts. One writes when he can no longer act. Writing you will be-lie truths. Renouncing the benefit of oblivion. Digging the hole that one is. Wrenching from the depths what has been buried there by the action of so much time. Yes, but can I be sure of wrenching free what is or what is not? I don't know, I don't know. To perform the insignificant titanically is also one way of acting. Even if it's backward. The only thing I'm sure about is that these Notes are addressed to no one. . . . This is a balancing of accounts. (*Y*, 53)

As is true with so many aspects of *I, the Supreme*, the basic structure of the novel is deceptive. Or, at best, it is a structure that must be considered on more than one level. Unlike the traditional historical novel, Roa's work is not event-oriented: all of the events that are alluded to have already taken place and are re-created, not by the "outer" novelistic text, but by Francia's recollections of them as he writes and dictates. Thus the entire content of the novel (notes and appendix aside) is retrospective, a direct consequence of the fact that Francia is speaking from the point of view of both the final days of life and from death itself. Also unlike the traditional historical novel *I, the Supreme* is far removed from the conventions of chronology. Francia moves effortlessly backward and forward in time from one event to another, relating them on the basis of intrinsic characteristics rather than temporal or spacial sequences. The segmental continuity of the novel, moreover, is based on large blocks of topics that are different in nature (the political versus the personal, the factual versus fantasy) and unrelated chronologically. The only link between them is that they form part of the vast subconsciousness of the dictator. Thus, one block deals with Francia's handling of foreign representatives who attempt to thwart his rule, another deals with the twin mysteries of his parentage and his education in France during the height of the Enlightenment, while another deals with his assessment of the accomplishments of his government. The novel in this way fails to follow an arrangement dictated by objective historical chronology.

At the same time the novel is also static in the complete absence of any developmental narrative. Like so many examples of the Latin American new novel, *I, the Supreme* is a single verbal complex that cannot be understood as the accumulation of the sense of a narrative trajectory. We grasp a total meaning, the total sense of a unitary "sign," to use a semiological concept. While the work is composed of parts (untitled chapters, untitled subdivisions, notes, individual paragraphs, sentences, words), the characteristics that the compiler attributes to Francia's "Notebooks" apply to the novel as a whole: a labyrinth of words that do not describe events, but a single consciousness of them. It is important to note that the entire work is an ecphrasis—the elaboration of a commentary—on an opening document, a spurious announcement by the dictator as to his "funeral arrangments." Fancia orders Patiño to uncover the identity of the forger; in the meantime the document sets in motion the complex maze of recollections and pronouncements that make up the ensuing four-hundred-page text. Patiño, of course, is never able to identify the hoaxer and the reader readily suspects that it is one of Francia's own scribblings. Whether the document as Roa presents it (it is printed in a facsimile of nineteenth-century script) really exists or not—and it is probable that it does—within the structure of the novel it is the immediate catalyst for the torrent of words that spill forth as Francia analyzes it, denounces it and begins to detail the reasons behind it and the man it mocks:

> I, THE SUPREME DICTATOR OF THE REPUBLIC,
> ORDER THAT UPON MY DEATH MY BODY BE DECAPITATED,
>   THE HEAD PLACED ON A PIKE FOR THREE DAYS IN THE
>   PLAZA DE LA REPUBLICA, TO WHERE THE CITIZENRY
>   WILL BE SUMMONED BY THE BELLS RUNG AT FULL
>   PEAL.
> ALL OF MY CIVIL AND MILITARY SERVANTS WILL BE
>   HANGED. THEIR BODIES WILL BE BURIED IN PASTURES

OUTSIDE THE CITY, WITHOUT CROSSES OR ANY OTHER
MARKER GIVING THEIR NAMES.
AT THE END OF THE PERIOD SPECIFIED, I ORDER THAT MY
REMAINS BE BURNED AND THAT THE ASHES BE
THROWN INTO THE RIVER. . . .
Where was this found? Nailed to the door of the Cathedral, Excellency. (*Y*,
7)

Thus, although we are from the ouset confronted with a document
that plays a crucial role in the structure of *I, the Supreme*, it is clear
that the documentary sources are part of the novelistic illusion itself,
the catalysts for the complex web of texts and voices that constitute
Roa's work.

IV   *Myth and "Writing Degree Zero"*

One of the most pliant concepts of modern literary scholarship is
the mythic. For the literary historian it has meant the study of the
transmission of stock narratives or motifs taken from canonical
sources of classical literature (for example, Ovid's *Metamorphoses*).
For the new critic the mythic referred to how the superficial
differences of literary works mask underlying universal preoccupations; these preoccupations are evident in the tales that reelaborate
them in ever-new guises and that are examined in alternately
anthropologic, folkloric, and psychoanalytic terms.

In more current usage, however, the mythic has taken on less
mystical connotations. Following the lead of Claude Lévi-Strauss's
"structural anthropology," literary structuralism views myths as
neutral creations. [7] Anthropologically speaking, a myth is the ad-hoc
creation of a people or an individual in the attempt to explain an
aspect of the complex human experience. These myths evince three
primordial features: (1) an explanation is attempted of the unexplain-
able, of the unknowable; thus, myths are always partial accounts,
although their internal complexity may appear to be impressive, and
they are ultimately failures because they attempt to reduce to
comprehension that which forever eludes us; (2) myths are narrative
in nature: at least they are narrative models on the basis of which
"stories" can be generated; (3) myths are arbitrary in nature: since
they are futile attempts at grasping the incomprehensible, the
structures of myths are at best parallel to the phenomena they
pretend to explain, although it is more likely that they are simply
irrelevant tangential approximations. We contemplate in the end the

myth rather than the experience that it attempts to explain and content ourselves with the secure belief that, thanks to the myth, we have found meaning.

For the new novel and the criticism that it has engendered, this anthropological concept of myth has held powerful sway. It is not difficult to understand how the cultural manifestations of so-called civilized society serve the same function as the anonymous myths of the "primitive mind." This seems particularly true of the narrative: the signed novel may be seen as superficially homologous with the anonymous myth. Both are complex constructs that aspire toward an ultimate comprehension that is denied them. However the signed novel, at least as it is currently being written, enjoys an ironic self-awareness not to be found in the collective myth. For the novelist is only too aware of the limitations of his mythopoeic endeavor, of how his elaborate verbal structures in the end signify not a higher meaning but only themselves and their own irremediable limitations. Within the contemporary Latin American novel we can point to numerous works that are mythic in their complex revelations of circumstance and event. Yet these novels are also equally ironic because they signal to the reader that these revelations are in the end only words that signify the absence of ultimate meaning. Hence the self-mocking interpretations of Ernesto Sabato's *On Heroes and Tombs* (especially in part 3, "Memorandum on The Blind") or Borges's short stories.[8] Or the "self-annihilating" (because ephemeral) texts of Gabriel García Márquez's *One Hundred Years of Solitude* or José Donoso's *The Obscene Bird of Night*. In short, these novels are mythic in their realization that all narrative explanations are rendered valid by man's compelling need to explain himself and to explain the universe to himself. They are also rendered presumptuous and impotent by virtue of the limitations placed on man's understanding.

In the case of Roa's novel, we are once again confronted with at least two levels: that of *I, the Supreme* as a literary text and that of Francia's dictations/scribblings as personal documents. As far as the level of novels is concerned, several aspects confirm Roa's adherence to the conception of the novel as futile myth. Roa is in a direct sense engaged in an effort to "understand" the enigmatic figure of Gaspar Francia, Paraguay's quite literally Perpetual Dictator. In an unsophisticated sense, we could see Roa working out an understanding of Francia for himself and then presenting that "interpretation" as the "thesis" of his novel. This is certainly what we would expect to find in a popular novel on so intriguing a historical personage. Yet it is abundantly clear that Roa has no such pretensions: the efforts to absent himself from the text (Francia's omnipresent voice and the mask of the "Compiler"), the use of documentary materials, the nonlinear and contradictory construction of the text, the disclaimers of the colophon are all indicators of inconclusiveness of the mythic narrative.

On a more interesting level, however, the "inner texts"—Francia's verbal proliferation—are equally mythic. Francia, as we see him creating texts, is also elaborating myths, vain attempts at self-identification and self-understanding. But as his words show, the dictator like the author knows full well that his luxuriant verbal artifacts are only that—artifacts. In the end they crumble under the burden of their presumed validity:

When I dictate to you, the words have one meaning; another when you write them down. Thus we are speaking two different languages. One is more at ease in the company of a dog he doesn't know than in that of a man who speaks an unknown language. False language is much more sociable than silence. Even my dog Sultán died taking with him to his grave the secret of what he was saying. What I want to ask of you, my esteemed Panzancho, is that when I dictate to you you won't try to artificialize the nature of things, but that you will naturalize what is artificial about the words. You are my ex-creting secretary. You write down what I dictate to you as if you yourself were speaking to the paper for me in secret. I want there to be something of me in what you write. I am not dictating to you a story on trivialities. Stories of entertainment. I am not dictating to you one of those real novels where the writer has illusions concerning the sacred character of literature. False priests of the written word make of their works literate ceremonies. In them, the characters have fantasies about reality or about language. They appear to celebrate the office decked out in supreme authority, but in reality they are upset when confronted with the figures that flow from their hands that they believe they are creating. Where craft becomes vice. Anyone who pretends to tell the story of his life becomes lost in what is too close to him. One can only speak of someone else. I can only manifest itself through Him. I do not speak to myself. I listen to myself through Him. I'm trapped in a tree. The tree calls out in its own way. Who can possibly know that it is I calling out, trapped inside it? Therefore, I demand from you the most absolute of silences, the utmost of secrets. By the same token, it is impossible to communicate anything to someone who is on the outside of the tree. He will hear the tree calling out. He will not hear the other call. My call. Do you understand? No? So much the better. (*Y*, 65; this passage contains several puns and no attempt has been made to render them with English equivalents.)

Roa's novel, as are those new novels that can be called self-mocking literary myths, is unquestionably an example of what Roland Barthes calls "writing degree zero."[9] For Barthes writing degree zero[10] means the production of literary texts that deny the dangerous pretensions of traditional modes of literary style and rhetoric. The latter are dangerous because they claim for literature a virtue and a pragmatic efficacy that is chimerical and because they adduce for literature an aesthetic goal that is in reality a neutralizing artificiality: any literature is dangerous that claims to provide ultimate interpretations of human experience. Writing is essentially a novelistic poetics that stresses the aesthetic humility of the literary text, the problematics of the "meanings" that emerge from texts that attempt to grapple with experience on its own ambiguous and elusive terms, and the complete expressive liberation of the writer from stylistic conventions predicated on the false notion of the stable and absolutist nature of language.

A major notion of Barthes's *écriture* (the French word is far more expressive than its English equivalent, "writing") is that we can no longer accept a concept of language—and hence of literature, which is composed of language—that maintains the fiction of a transparent relationship between speaker, message, and receptor. That is to say, the illusion that I have a clear meaning to communicate, that I choose a transparent message to communicate it (transparent in the sense of immediately comprehensible and unambiguous) and that this message is received and understood without problem by the receptor. In literature this fiction has meant a school of criticism that insists that the "meaning" of a work of literature is accessible and that, in the final analysis, only one meaning is appropriate to the text. Barthes, of course, would not only reject this notion of one primordial meaning, but he would also question seriously the idea that a text has any overt meaning whatever to communicate. What it does do is communicate itself: the unique meaning of a text is the text itself. All other meanings are created by the reader from that text. That is, the reader does not receive the meaning of the text, but rather he attributes to it a meaning he believes it to have. There are many key quotes that could be given from Barthes; the following, chosen by Hugh M. Davidson, is as revealing as any:

Let us pose first of all the image of a triumphant plural which is not impoverished by any constraint of representation (or imitation). In this ideal text, the networks are multiple with an interplay among them such that no network dominates the others; this text is a galaxy of signifiers, not a structure of signifieds; it has no beginning; it is reversible; one has access to it by several entries, none of which can be declared with certainty to be the principal one; the codes that it mobilizes extend their profiles as far as one can see—they are undecidable (the sense is never submitted to a decisive principle, unless it be by a throw of dice): systems of sense may take hold of this absolutely plural text, but the number of these systems is never closed, having as their measure the infinity of language.[11]

Davidson goes on to comment: "This ideal text has no exterior to be outlined; it has no totality: insofar as we can speak of narrative structure or of narrative grammar and logic apropos of a text, we are concerned with incomplete or parsimonious plurality"[12]

Barthes's concept of writing has many inherent flaws, as does any critical position. However, more than as an intellectual framework for the criticism of contemporary literature, Barthes's position has been important as the catalyst for a particular conception of literature among writers themselves. That is to say, Barthes's writing may be more influential in the writing of literature than in the criticism of it, which should not be surprising, since the term writing does, in fact, direct our attention more to the compositional aspects of literature.

In the case of Roa's novel we have already alluded to certain features that can be seen as the realization of Barthian writing: the illusion of the absent or inconsequential author, the interplay between "real" texts and fictional texts, the contradictory nature of large portions of Francia's texts (as noted by the "Compiler"; see above); the absence of linear structure and ths presence of a series of texts whose interrelationship depends less on the formal link between one segment and another and more on their status as a series of expanding ecphrases of the initial text (the forged proclamation); the denial not only of narrative chronology, but of "real" world distinctions such as life and death and past/present/future. All of these characteristics are employed by Roa for the apparent purpose of thwarting the desire of the naive reader to reduce his text to a definitive interpretation of Francia's regime. Undoubtedly there will be those critics who perceive in Roa's work the attempt to present a categorical interpretation of the Supreme Dictator, and they will write critical evaluations accordingly. Their evaluations will present revelations of the novel's underlying meaning and judicial assessments in accord with the degree of agreement with the proposed revelations. *I, the Supreme* will unquestionably be the object of political interpretations, although, as the insistence on the novel as an example of Barthian writing means to show, such interpretations will necessarily go against the novel's very nature.[13]

The allegedly mythic quality of *I, the Supreme* is a further confirmation of the interest in presenting a verbal profile of Francia, but not an interpretation. If Francia's own texts are mythic in the ultimately futile quest for a self-interpretation, Roa's novels is mythic in its adduction of a verbal structure that presents Francia's quest. That structure is the form of the novel as we receive it, although it is a structure that cannot be reduced to an absolute meaning. Like anthropological myths, the structure of a new novel like Roa's has the "meaning" of its form (the text signifies itself), but the possibility of hermeneutics on the basis of a fixed system of meaning is denied. It is by virtue of this denial that we associate with examples of Barthian writing a display of language that seems to be so much meaningless sound (compare Barthes's quasi-motto: "writing is the spectacular commitment of language").[14] Although Roa does not go as far as Severo Sarduy in creating a novelistic language that denies any reference to conventional systematic semantics, Francia's verbomania, his use of puns, his continual contradiction or correction of what he has already uttered, all contribute to the denial of ultimate meaning. The reader is in the end forced to remain contemplating Francia's "spectacular commitment of language" (his extravagant puns, for example) because that language impedes rather than facilitates access to any putative underlying meaning.

If all human linguistic expression, whether colloquial or literary, is in the last analysis either meaningless or polysemous (and an infinity of meaning is tantamount of the negation of meaning), language is self-defeating. Hence the recurring metaphor in the Latin American new novel of the destruction of the text: a whirlwind carries away the text of García Márquez's *One Hundred Years of Solitude;* the narrator of Donoso's *The Obscene Bird of Night* is bundled into a sack with other rubbish and burnt as firewood; Ernesto Sabato, the writer who appears in Ernesto Sabato's *Abaddón the Exterminator,* ends up contemplating a blank sheet of paper jammed in a typewriter that he no longer has the strength to operate anyway; and so on. In Roa's novel the destruction of text comes with Francia's realization of the futility of his attempt at self-knowledge and self-justification. In the conversation with the dog Sultán, which Francia is in the process of transcribing as it takes place, the former denounces the absurdity of the dictator's undertaking and prophesies the destruction of his Words. As befits a man preoccupied with his place in history and with the correspondence between his individual memory and the collective unconscious of his people, destruction will take the form of aphasia accompanied by the deterioration of linguistic competence:

First you will forget nouns, then adjectives, even interjections. In your great outbursts of anger at best you will still be able to articulate a few phrases, the vaguest possible. For example, you used to say "I want, which means to be able to say I don't want." Before too long when you attempt to assert NO, you will only be able to stammer out, after many starts and at a pitch of annoyance, "I can't say NO!"

You will begin with pronouns. Do you have any idea of what it will mean for you not to be able to remember, not to be able to stutter more than I-HE? Your suffering will be over fast. In the end you won't even be able to remember. . . [my ellipsis].

From the one side you will be bombarded by idiotic sounds from a foreign language. An extinct language that revives for a moment as it is cut to shreds by your scissors-tongue. From the other side, unknown images. You will continue to see some objects. You will not be able to see the letters of books, nor of what you are writing. Which will not keep you from copying; nor even from imitating the letter of a strange alphabet, but without being able to understand a thing. I am writing, you will say, as though my eyes were closed, even though I know they are wide open. It will be a beautiful experience for you. Your last. If you feel bored, you can play dominoes or cards with Patiño; even beat him as many times as you like.

Listen to me, Sultán. . . .

I know, I know; you don't need to tell me a thing, ex-Supreme one. Everything about you is crystal-clear to me. You want to write. (*Y*, 419; ellipsis in text.)

In the end Francia comes face to face with the realization that even the utterances of a Supreme Dictator are meaningless. One of the recurring images of the novel is the imperfect state of the documents on which it is based. On several dozen occasions segments of the novel end with phrases like "the rest is illegible," "a page is missing," "what comes next is blotted out," "the bottom-half has been burned away," and so on. It is therefore fitting that the novel end on just such a note. Once again, the words are self-accusatory and stress the absolute finality of the lack of knowledge gained. After a tirade of mockery, the novel ends with the words: "That's the way things are. How about it, Supreme Deceased, if we leave you like that, condemned to perpetual hunger . . . [my ellipsis], because you didn't know . . . (*pasted over, the rest illegible, the remainder not to be found, the worm-eaten words of the Book scattered to the four winds*) (*Y*, 456; ellipsis and italics in text).

V *Conclusion*

The foregoing presentation of *I, the Supreme* has only scratched the surface of an extremely dense and complex novel. Indeed, many basic aspects of structure have not even been dealt with (for example, much needs to be said about Francia's I-He doubling). But what can be stressed by way of summation is the quality of the novel that arises from the successful utilization of a number of features corresponding of Barthian writing, in particular the amalgam of document and fiction and the resistence to converting the work into a politically based (or biased) interpretation of Francia the historical figure. Some will denounce Roa's novel for its denial of political readings, but many too will accept it for the outstanding accomplishment it purports to bè: a literary text.

CHAPTER 6

Conclusions

T HE Augusto Roa Bastos presented in this study can be approached from a number of converging perspectives. There is Roa the short story writer and novelist who, in turning from poetry to fiction, provided Paraguay with its first major prose writer. Although Roa would himself consider it presumptuous to date important Paraguayan fiction from the beginning of his own success with the short story and novel, it is unquestionable that young and promising Paraguayan writers can point to a national model that has attained international recognition.

Roa Bastos is also the model of the Latin American exile. One might want to speak of the linguistic exile, isolated from the popular language of his people, Guaraní, and resigned to the need to express himself in what may still be considered in many sectors of Latin America the language of feudal oppression, Spanish. At least it is an international language that, although Roa has shown how it can be molded to reflect popular forms of expression without becoming regionalistic, distances the writer from the masses of his people who do not claim it as their native language. One could also speak in the same vein of the tensions of a physical exile in which the writer is separated from one very distinct national reality—rural Paraguay— and forced to live and write within the context of a very different one—cosmopolitan Buenos Aires. After twenty-five years of resi- dence in Buenos Aires, Roa is still unable to accept wholly its life-style. Although no nostalgic romantic in his literary vision of Paraguay, it is unquestionable that Roa sees his country, its tradi- tions, and its life-style, from the perspective of his exile within an essentially alien culture. One notes that the juxtaposition of Paraguayan and Buenos Aires values is nowhere more evident than in his use of nineteenth-century historical materials in *I, the Supreme*. In terms of these two circumstances, which can either be accepted as basic facts in a writer's biography to be given no more than their due emphasis in identifying him, or which can be blown up into putative psychological parameters of his creative work, the circumstances of his political exile—one more Latin American forced to flee the persecution of an unrelenting dictatorship—seem somewhat prosaic.

We can speak in a more literary context of Roa as exemplary of the contemporary writer of a fiction of social criticism and protest. Unlike the socialist realism of the 1930s, recent fiction dealing with the plight of man oppressed by dictatorial regimes is less denunciatory in an overt manner and more concerned with the nature of human existence within the context of oppression. For this reason, there is little in the way of specific political denunciation in *Son of Man*. Yet the context is unmistakable, and the creation of a number of major figures that represent the nature and extent of human suffering in a world that denies their very humanity is what makes the work acceptable as fiction rather than as a political tract. Moreover, the use of mythic perspectives—figures that unconsciously bear profound interrelationships with each other and with their sociohistorical circumstances—identifies Roa Bastos with writers like Miguel Ángel Asturias, José María Arguedas, and Juan Rulfo. These writers have recognized the limitations of outdated variations on nineteenth-century realism and documentary regionalism (Creolism, indigenism, local color) and have perceived the advantages of a mythopoeic literature emphasizing the underlying immutable relationships between men and events rather than the surface texture of the flow of daily life. Even in the more recent fiction that is identified as the *nueva narrativa* (the new fiction or new narrative), while there is less of an interest in "poetic myths," we can still point to a mythopoeic process that continues the interest in representative figures and events with a far-reaching meaning for the identification of the significant patterns of the Latin American experience.

Finally, as an extension of the comments of the preceding paragraph, it is possible to stress Roa's accomplishments within the aesthetics of current Latin American fiction. Literary criticism has progressed far beyond the historical practice of assessing a writer's accomplishments in terms of his "originality" and his "unique contributions" to the development of a literary tradition. No longer accepting as particularly valid the romantic emphasis on individual accomplishments and subjective fulfillment in art, critical opinion is satisfied to recognize in an author the successful creation of literary objects. Thus one could speak of original characteristics in *Son of Man*, where Roa combines an unmistakable political position with the creation of mythic figures, or the singularness of *I, the Supreme* as the first Latin American novel to treat a legendary dictator in terms of the illusion of a totally documentary fiction. Yet what is more at issue is the identification in the writer of the underlying premises of his work and, subsequently, the assessment of the degree of his success in elaborating those premises in terms of the structural conventions that he has chosen. Of course the identification of the original contributions of a writer's work is objective in a positivistic sense (we can document the first Latin American novel to use Guaraní expressions, for example), while the assessment of the efficacy of an author's structural elaborations of fiction is subject, not to demonstration, but only to reasonable assertion.

In modern fiction one is less constrained to identify "brilliant" writers. Few of these exist, and it is my own opinion that, if brilliance can in fact be identified in fiction, Roa is indisputably brilliant. But today when the literary marketplace is flooded with literature, when fiction proliferates as the most basic of all literary modalities for the modern reader, to assert the adequacy of the writer's literary structures is considerable praise in itself. Whatever the final approach to Roa Bastos's fiction will be within future historical assessments of the Latin American novel, the touchstone of his current importance among both academic critics and fellow writers is above all else the singular structural adequacy of his fictional works.

Notes and References

Chapter One

1. Rubén Bareiro Saguier (professor of Guaraní language and culture at the Sorbonne), also an exile, has written on the theme of the exile in Paraguayan literature: "El tema del exilio en la narrativa paraguaya contemporánea," *Caravelle*, no. 14 (1970), 79–96.

2. Bareiro Saguier's harrassment by the Paraguayan government is reviewed with extensive documentation in "Serie Los marginados. III. Caso Bareiro Saguier," *Hispamérmica*, nos. 4–5 (1973), 73–101. It is a minicasebook study of the rigors of being an artist and intellectual in some parts of Latin America today.

3. While there are small publishing operations in Paraguay and Argentina that have printed Paraguayan literature, the only hope for recognition lies in publishing with those houses that have promoted the best of the younger Paraguayan writers: Editorial Losada, Centro Editor de América Latina, Editorial Sudamericana, all located in Buenos Aires. To the best of my knowledge, neither Joaquín Mortiz in México nor Seix Barral (and its splinter, Barral) in Barcelona, houses that have done much to promote the new Latin American fiction, have published Paraguayan authors.

4. Biographical information on Roa is scant and somewhat difficult to come by, since he chooses a life of relative anonymity. I am grateful for the information that Roa and his wife, Amelia Hannois, supplied to me. I have in addition drawn upon material contained in Lilí Olga Trevisán, "Literatura de una tierra joyosa. Su novelista: Augusto Roa Bastos," *Revista de literaturas modernas*, no. 6 (1967), 79–107.

5. Unlike some of his more "public-oriented" Latin American companions in literary arms, Roa grants very few interviews. One of the most interesting is the one with Günter Lorenz, which took place during the 1967 Latin American Writers Workshop in Berlin. While the interview remains generally cordial, Roa refuses to be maneuvered into facile statements and a pat position. In a personal communication Roa has insisted that the printed text does not faithfully reflect his conversations with Lorenz. It should be noted that the conversations were first recorded in Spanish, published in German translation, and only subsequently in Spanish. See Günter Lorenz, "Augusto Roa Bastos," in *Diálogo con Latinoamérica, panorama de una lireratura del futuro* (Santiago, Chile: Editorial Pomaire, 1972), pp. 271–310.

6. David Maldavsky, "Autocrítica: reportaje a Augusto Roa Bastos," *Los libros,* no. 12 (1970), 11. For a somewhat different perspective on the bilingual conflict, see Josefina Pla, "Español y guaraní en la intimidad de la cultura paraguaya," *Caravelle,* no. 14 (1970), 7–21. Pla presents a historical perspective on the relative fortunes of the two languages in Paraguay; unlike Roa, who is more sensitive to the tensions of the synchronic interplay of Guaraní and Spanish, Pla concludes on the traditional liberal note that Paraguay will remain backward and oppressed until Spanish truly dominates, replacing the Guaraní promoted by self-serving status quo interests(!). Roa has written a number of papers on the conflicts and tensions of Paraguayan society, particularly as reflected in language and in literature. Three of the best are; "Pasión y expresión de la literatura paraguaya," *Universidad* (Santa Fe), no. 44 (1960), 157–74; "Crónica paraguaya," *Sur,* no. 293 (1965), 102–12; "Entretiens: Augusto Roa Bastos," *Caravelle,* no. 17 (1971), 207–18.

7. Hugo Rodríguez Alcalá describes this early poetry in the first part of his study "Augusto Roa Bastos y *El trueno entre las hojas,*" *Revista iberoamericana,* no. 39 (1955), 19–45.

8. Maldavsky, p. 11.

9. Roa Bastos, "Entretiens . . . ," p. 218.

10. There are two fundamental studies on Paraguayan history and civilization: George Pendle, *Paraguay, a Riverside Nation,* 3d ed. (London: Oxford University Press, 1970); and Efraím Cardozo, *Breve historia del Paraguay* (Bueno Aires: Editorial Universidad de Buenos Aires, 1965).

11. One of the earliest essays on Francia was written by Thomas Carlyle, "Dr. Francia," *Foreign Quarterly Review* 31 (1843), 544–89. Carlyle's gothic interest in Francia and the attraction-repulsion of his dark figure are reflected well in his closing words:

In this manner, all being yet dark and void for European eyes, have we to imagine that the man Rodríguez Francia passed, in a remote, but highly remarkable, not unquestionable or unquestioned manner, across the confused theatre of this world. For some thirty years, he was all the government of his native Paraguay could be said to have. For some six-and-twenty years he was express Sovereign with bared sword, stern as Rhadamanthus: through all his years, and through all his days, since the beginning of him, a Man or Sovereign of iron energy and industry, of great and severe labour. So lived Dictator Francia, and had no rest; and only in Eternity any prospect of rest. A Life of terrible labour;—but for the last twenty years, the Fulgencio Plot being once torn in pieces, and all now quiet under him it was a more equable labour; Severe but equable, as that of a hardly draught-steed fitted in his harness; no longer plunging and champing; but pulling steadily—till he do all his rough miles, and get to his still *home.*

. . . He is dead, this remarkable Francia; there is no doubt about it: have not we and our readers heard pieces of his Funeral Sermon! He died on the 20th of September 1840, as the Rev. Pérez informs us; the people crowding round his Government House with much emotion, nay "with tears," as Pérez will have it. Three Excellencies succeeded him; as some "Directorate," "Junta Gubernativa," or whatever the name of it is, before whom this reverend Pérez preaches. God preserve them for many years.

Quoted from Paul Kramer and Robert E. McNicoll, *Latin American Panorama* (New York: Putnam's, 1968), p. 168.

12. Hugo Rodríguez-Alcalá, *Historia de la literatura paraguaya* (Mexico City: Ediciones de Andrea, 1970), pp. 20–21.

Chapter Two

1. *El trueno entre las hojas,* 2d ed. (Buenos Aires: Editorial Losada, 1961); hereafter cited in the text as *T*.

2. There are two basic papers on "magical realism": Ángel Flores, "Magical Realism in Spanish American Fiction," *Hispania* 38 (1955), 187–201; and Luis Leal, "El realismo mágico en la literatura hispanoamericana," *Cuadernos americanos,* no. 153 (1967), 230–35. While it is questionable whether from the perspective of today and the general prevalence of nonnaturalistic modes of fiction magical realism should be given autonomy as a special modality of mid-century Latin American literature, it is undeniable that the term served as a rallying point for the development of the contemporary narrative.

3. There are a number of superficial reviews on *Thunder,* indicating that the collection received more attention when it was published than is normal for the first book of a Latin American author. However, the only extensive studies are Hugo Rodríguez Acalá, "Augusto Roa Bastos y *El trueno entre las hojas,*" *Revista iberoamericana,* no. 39 (1955), 19–45; Mabel Piccini, "*El trueno entre las hojas* y el humanismo revolucionario," *Cuadernos del Instituto de Literatura Argentina e Iberoamericana,* no. 1 (1965), 6–15; amd Adelfo León Aldana, *La cuentística de Augusto Roa Bastos* (Montevideo: Ediciones Geminis, 1975). Additional studies are listed in the Selected Bibliography.

4. Rodríguez Alcalá, p. 29.

5. Hugo Rodríguez Alcalá has studied this story in "Jorge Luis Borges en 'La excavación', de Augusto Roa Bastos," in *El cuento hispanoamericano ante la crítica,* ed. Enrique Pupo-Walker (Madrid: Editorial Castalia, 1973), pp. 179–94. The assertions that the story manifests Roa's interest in Borges's concerns with the cyclical nature of time and the multiple nature of events are, however, unconvincing: both the texture and the underlying meaning of Roa's story are far removed from Borges's work.

Chapter Three

1. *Hijo de hombre* (Buenos Aires: Editorial Losada, 1960).

2. Concerning the Christian symbolism of *Son of Man,* see in particular Urte Lehnerdt, "Ensayo de interpretación de *Hijo de hombre* a través de su simbolismo cristiano y social," *Revista iberoamericana* 34 (1968), 67–83; and Clara Passafari de Gutiérrez, "La condición humana en la narrativa de Roa Bastos," *Universidad* (Santa Fe), no. 46 (1960), 137–61.

3. Hugo Rodríguez Alcalá, *"Hijo de hombre,* de Roa Bastos y la intrahistoria del Paraguay," *Cuadernos americanos,* no. 121 (1963), 221–34. See also Andris Kleinbergs, "Estudio estructural de *Hijo de hombre,* de Roa Bastos," *Atenea,* no. 420 (1968), 155–67.

4. Quoted passages are from *Son of Man,* trans. Rachel Caffyn (London: Gollancz, 1965); hereafter cited in text as *H.*

5. Jan Lechner, "Apuntes para el estudio de la prosa de Roa Bastos," *Norte* 12, no. 2 (1971), 28–34, has failed to see this distinction and appears to believe that all Christ figures must be orthodoxically Christian; on this basis he complains on the "misunderstanding" in the use of "Christ figure" in David W. Foster, *The Myth of Paraguay in the Fiction of Augusto Roa Bastos* (Chapel Hill: University of North Carolina Press, 1969). To comprehend the extent to which modern Christ figures may be antiinstitutionally Christian, consult Edwin M. Moseley, *Pseudonyms of Christ in the Modern Novel; Motifs and Methods* (Pittsburgh: University of Pittsburgh Press, 1963); and Theodore Zilkowski, *Fictional Transfigurations of Jesus* (Princeton: Princeton University Press, 1972). For a mythic reading of *Son of Man,* see Adriana Valdés and Ignacio Rodríguez, *"Hijo de hombre:* el mito como fuerza social," *Taller de letras,* no. 1 (1971), 75–95; and Humberto E. Robles, "El círculo y la cruz en *Hijo de hombre," Nueva narrativa hispanoamericana* 4 (1974), 193–219.

6. Concerning the first chapter of the novel, see David W. Foster, "The Figure of Christ Crucified as a Narrative Symbol of Roa Bastos' *Hijo de hombre," Books Abroad* 37 (1963), 16–20; and Esperanza Gurza, "Gaspar ha muerto. ¡Viva el Cristo!" *La palabra y el hombre,* no. 43 (1967), 499–505.

7. Roa has been criticized for more than one "lapse" into historical inaccuracy in his books, but nowhere as vociferously as in reference to this chapter on the "War of Thirst." In José Justo Prieto, "Entrevista a Gabriel Casaccia y a Augusto Roa Bastos," *Alcor,* nos. 18–19 (August, 1962), 6–8, the author defends himself by reminding critics of the poetic licenses that novelists are allowed to take in the furtherance of their metaphoric interpretations of events: "More than the historical anecdote in itself, I have been interested in its 'intrahistoric' [that is, underlying or abstract] meaning."

8. This section is based on David W. Foster, "Una nota sobre el punto de vista narrativo en *Hijo de hombre* de Roa Bastos," *Revista iberoamericana* 36 (1970), 643–50. Jean L. Andreu, "Hijo *de homre,* fragmentatción y unidad," *Revista iberoamericana,* nos. 96–97 (1976), 473–83, covers essentially the same ground.

9. Seymour Menton, "Realismo mágico y dualidad en *Hijo de hombre," Revista iberoamericana* 33 (1967), 55–70.

10. Foster, *The Myth of Paraguay in the Fiction of Augusto Roa Bastos.*

11. See above, note 3.

12. Modern criticism would not see it as necessary that this essay concern itself with Roa's own observations, contained in a personal letter, that (1) he was unaware himself that there was an alternation in tone between the

chapters, and (2) that he personally is of the opinion that "the author is both the hero and the antihero *par excellence* of his own works." However, Roa also recognized that the author is the one least qualified to interpret his own works. This is reasonable—and it is a belief shared by most serious critics—since the author still "lives" his works too subjectively.

13. For a somewhat different perspective on the rhetorical problems of the novel, seen as essentially unresolved, see David Maldavsky, "Un enfoque semiótico de la narrativa de Roa Bastos: *Hijo de hombre*," in *Homenaje a Augusto Roa Bastos,* ed. Helmy F. Giacoman (Long Island City, N.Y.: Las Américas, 1973), pp. 79–95. Rubén Bareiro Saguier, "Noción del personaje en *Hijo de hombre*," *Nueva narrativa hispanoamericana* 4 (1974), 69–74, also writes from a semiotic point of view. His position, with which the present study agrees, is that the characters of a novel must be seen not as "psychological" wholes, but as exponents of literary functions within the overall structure of the novel.

Chapter Four

1. See the titles in the listing of Roa's recent short fiction in the Selected Bibliography. Roa has also written a children's story: *El pollito de fuego,* illus. Juan Marchesi (Buenos Aires: Ediciones de la Flor, 1974). There is a review by David W. Foster in *Books Abroad* 50 (1976), 125–26.

2. The four collections are: *El baldío* (Buenos Aires: Editorial Losada, 1966); *Los pies sobre el agua* (Buenos Aires: Centro Editor de América Latina, 1967); *Moriencia* (Caracas: Monte Ávila, 1969); and *Cuerpo presente* (Buenos Aires: Centro Editor de América Latina, 1971). Of these, *Moriencia* is the most complete and serves as the basis for this chapter. Three important review articles on these stories are Humberto Becacece, " . . . *Moriencia* . . . ," *Sur,* no. 320 (1967), 95–98; Alfredo Andrés, "Ese complejo ser paraguayo [on *El baldío*]," *Sur,* no. 306 (1967), 58–60; and Fernando Aínsa, "Un realismo de la imaginación [on *El baldío*[," *Mundo nuevo,* no. 11 (1967), 78–80. The thematic range of Roa's fiction is examined by Jaime Herszenhorn, "Reflexiones sobre la temática de los cuentos de Augusto Roa Bastos," in *Homenaje a Augusto Roa Bastos,* pp. 251–66.

3. At least in Europe and the United States. But the uncertain critical position of such Argentine journals as *Los libros* or *Latinoamericana* (both ceased publication in the mid-1970s) indicate that there is no universal rejection of socialist realism in Latin America. Yet both *Mundo nuevo* (Paris and Buenos Aires; now ceased) and Octavio Paz's *Plural* (publication was suspended with Paz's departure in 1976) bespoke the best of mid-century criticism.

4. On Viñas's fiction, see Emir Rodríguez Monegal, "David Viñas, en su contorno," *Mundo nuevo,* no. 18 (1967), 75–84.

5. With reference to *Hijo de hombre,* David Maldavsky has written that "The counterposing of Spanish and Guaraní in this work is, in my opinion,

one of the clearest indications of a semantic-pragmatic contradiction. When this contradiction is no longer the case, as happens in the first five stories of *Moriencia*, which were written by the author ten years later, Guaraní appears as an implicit language to whose syntactic matrix he turns for the organization of his style in Spanish. Here we see how Guaraní and Spanish are not in conflict, but rather attain true aesthetic harmony" (p. 32), in his "Consideraciones sobre el nivel pragmático," *Problemas de literatura*, no. 2 (1972), 23–36.

6. See his own comments in "Entretiens: Augusto Roa Bastos," *Caravelle*, no. 17 (1971), 207–18. "But the Paraguayan of today—and, as a consequence, his cultural expression—lives immersed in that pathologic irreality of 'dis-realization' into which his history has coagulated" (p. 210).

7. The story is found in *Moriencia*, pp. 11–16. An early version of this section appeared as "*La pensée sauvage* in Augusto Roa Bastos' Recent Fiction," *Chasqui* 4, no. 2 (1975), 29–34.

8. *Moriencia*, pp. 12–13; hereafter cited in text as *M*.

9. This is, one will recall, the debilitating sentimental notion in "El trueno entre las hojas."

10. *Moriencia*, pp. 17–24.

11. Ibid., pp. 25–36.

12. Ibid., pp. 43–52.

13. "The proliferation of concepts, as in the case of technical languages, goes with more constant attention to properties of the world, with an interest that is more alert to possible distinctions which can be introduced between them. This thirst for objective knowledge is one of the most neglected aspects of the thought of people we call 'primitive.' Even if it is rarely directed towards facts of the same level as those with which modern science is concerned, it implies comparable intellectual application and methods of observation. In both cases the universe is an object of thought at least as much as it is a means of satisfying needs.

"Every civilization tends to overestimate the objective orientation of its thought and this tendency is never absent. When we make the mistake of thinking that the Savage is governed solely by organic or economic needs, we forget that he levels the same reproach at us, and that to him his own desire for knowledge seems more balanced than ours . . ." (Claude Lévi-Strauss, *The Savage Mind* [Chicago: University of Chicago Press, 1966], pp. 2–3; originally published in 1962 as *La pensée sauvage*).

14. On this concept see Mirea Eliade, *The Myth of the Eternal Return* (London: Routledge & Kegan Paul, 1955).

15. Frederic Jameson has summarized Lévi-Strauss's ideas in *Tristes tropiques* on man's need to create myths as follows: "Art, along with mythic narrative, may thus be seen as a working out in formal terms of what a culture is unable to resolve concretely; or, in our present terminology, we may say that for this view art is a sign-system, an articulation on the level of the signifier, or a signified which is essentially felt to be an antimony or a

contradiction" (*The Prison-House of Language* [Princeton: Princeton University Press, 1972], p. 162). While one may choose not to subscribe to this hypothesis as the basis for a critical theory, it may certainly be accepted as the basis for a very generalized aesthetic principle among contemporary writers. Whether Roa has consciously assimilated Lévi-Strauss is immaterial, for it is the critic's ability to identify him with this generalized principle that reveals in the structure of the story the mythopoeic drive and its rationale that Lévi-Strauss has recognized.

16. Ibid., pp. 55–62.

17. See Aínsa's comments in "Un realismo de la imaginación": "Exile, the theme of being obliged to live outside one's frontiers, can thus be proposed as the unifying thread for the collection of stories that make up *El baldío*" (p. 78). In *Moriencia* three stories make up this section, two of which—but not "Juegos nocturnos"—are contained in *El baldío*.

18. See David W. Foster, ". . . *El oscuro* . . . ," *Books Abroad* 43 (1969), 568.

19. Ibid., pp. 63–68.

20. Yet it has merited a separate analysis by Mario E. Ruiz, "La introspección auto-crítica en 'Contar un cuento.' " in *Homenje a Augusto Roa Bastos*, pp. 267–76.

21. *Moriencia*, pp. 69–81.

22. In various places in David W. Foster, *The Novels of Camilo José Cela* (Columbia, Mo.: University of Missouri Press, 1967).

23. *Moriencia*, pp. 86–102. The story is certainly difficult. But I cannot agree with Hugo Rodríguez Alcalá that "It appears that Roa set up for himself a series of technical difficulties that could illustrate and exhibit art, as an athlete in an obstacle course might wish to multiply the number of hurdles in order to show off the agility with which he overcomes them, seeking the public's applause," and my own analysis intends to demonstrate that much more than gratuitous narrative acrobatics—so anathematic to Roa's art—are involved. Hugo Rodríguez Alcalá, "Official Truth and 'True' Truth: Augusto Roa Bastos' 'Borrador de un informe,' " *Studies in Short Fiction* 8, no. 1 (1971), 141–54.

Chapter Five

1. Augusto Roa Bastos, *Yo el Supremo* (Buenos Aires: Siglo XXI Argentina, 1974); cited in the text as *Y*.

2. In a personal communication dated March 3, 1972, Roa speaks of Mario Vargas Llosa and Carlos Fuentes as having organized an *equipo* ("team") of writers to do an anthology of stories on Latin American dictators. In addition to the two compilers, Julio Cortázar, Roa Bastos, and Gabriel García Márquez were among those who were to contribute an original piece. When the anthology did not materialize (Latin American dictators are simply too monumental to be contained within the bounds of a short story), the

agreement was reached for each to write a novel. Whether the other authors mentioned in this context were, in addition to the five listed above, parties to the agreement is less significant than the fact that a "trend" or ' "constant" for the new novel had been established that would produce a series of works on dictators.

3. An earlier version of this section appeared as a review article, "Augusto Roa Bastos' *I, the Supreme:* the Image of a Dictator," *Latin American Literary Review,* no. 7 (1975), 31–35.

4. Hubert Herring, *A History of Latin America,* 2d rev. ed. (New York: Knopf, 1961), pp. 712–13.

5. See the sociologically based analysis of Domingo Miliani, "El dictador: objeto narrativo en *Yo el Supremo,"* *Revista de crítica literaria latinoamericana,* no. 4 (1976), 103–19. The following "exchange" also involves sociopolitical focuses, and Sarlo stresses the implications of Francia's verbomania: Beatriz Sarlo, *"Yo el Supremo:* el discurso del poder," *Los libros,* no. 37 (1974), 24–25; Antonio Carmona, *"Yo el Supremo,* ¿La escritura del poder o la impotencia de la escritura?" *Los libros,* no. 38 (1974), 30–31. Mario Benedetti also speaks in sociological terms in "El recurso del patriarca," *Revista de crítica literaria latinoamericana,* no. 3 (1976), 55–67.

6. These topics on the conventions of the novel are covered by Wayne C. Booth, *The Rhetoric of Fiction* (Chicago: University of Chicago Press, 1961). Unfortunately no really solid theoretical study exist on the conventions of the so-called new novel, although a number of works on French developments are available.

7. See Claude Lévi-Strauss, *Structural Anthropology* (New York: Basic Books, 1963). Concerning Lévi-Strauss's major theories, see Edmund Leach, *Claude Lévi-Strauss,* rev. ed. (New York: Viking Press, 1974). The French anthropologist's impact on literature is discussed by James A. Boon, *From Symbolism to Structuralism, Lévi-Strauss in a Literary Tradition* (New York: Harper and Row, 1972).

8. On Borges see David William Foster, "Borges and Structuralism: Toward an Implied Poetics," *Modern Fiction Studies* 19 (1973), 341–51.

9. Concerning this aspect of the new novel see Jaime Giordano's preliminary essay, "El nivel de la escritura en la narrativa hispanoamericana contemporánea," *Nueva narrativa hispanoamericana* 4 (1974), 307–44.

10. The term is taken from the title *Writing Degree Zero* (Boston: Beacon Press, 1970); originally published in French in 1953.

11. Roland Barthes, as quoted by Hugh M. Davidson, "Sign, Sense, and Barthes," in Seymour Chatman, *Approaches to Poetics* (New York: Columbia University Press, 1973), pp. 39–40. The quote, given in Davidson's own translation, is taken from Barthes's *S/Z* (Paris: Éditions du Seuil, 1970), pp. 11–12.

12. Ibid., p. 40.

13. The second part of *Writing Degree Zero,* "Political Modes of Writing," deals with the errors of political novels that pretend to provide "clear"

interpretations of sociopolitical phenomena. Needless to say, Barthes has been widely attacked for his rejection of the possibility of efficacious commitments in literature. His contention that the notion of a literary pragmatics is an inherent contradiction is unquestionably unacceptable to neo-Marxist and other sociological critics.

14. Quoted in *Writing Degree Zero,* p. 25.

Selected Bibliography

PRIMARY SOURCES

El baldío. Buenos Aires: Losada, 1966. Contents: "El baldío," "Contar un cuento," "Encuentro con el traidor," "La rebelión," "El aserradero," "Borrador de un informe," "La trijera," "Hermanos," "La flecha y la manzana," "El y el otro," "El pájaro mosca."

Cuerpo presente y otros cuentos. Bueno Aires: Centro Editor de América Latina, 1971. Contents: "Nonato," "Cuando un pájaro entierra sus plumas," "Función," "Moriencia," "Bajo el puente," "Cuerpo presente," "Macario," "Borrador de un informe," "Hogar," "La excavación."

Hijo de hombre. Buenos Aires: Losada, 1960. There are several subsequent editions under different imprints.

Madera quemada; cuentos. Santiago de Chile: Editorial Universitaria, 1967. Contents: "Kurupí," "Bajo el puente," "Niño-Azoté," "El baldío," "El y el otro," "El viejo Señor Obispo," "La excavación," "El prisionero," "La tumba viva," "El trueno entre las hojas."

Moriencia; cuentos. Caracas: Monte Ávila, 1969. Contents: *Moriencia:* "Moriencia," "Nonato," "Bajo el puente," "Ración de León," "Cuerpo presente." *Juegos nocturnos:* "Juegos nocturnos," "Contar un cuento," "El y el otro." *Borrador de un informe:* "Borrador de un informe," "Encuentro con el traidor," "El baldío," "El aserradero," "La flecha y la manzana," "El pájaro mosca," "La rebelión."

El naranjal ardiente, nocturno paraguayo. Asunción: Ed. Diálogo, 1960.

Los pies sobre el agua. Buenos Aires: Centro Editor de América Latina, 1967. Contents: "Nonato," "Macario," "Borrador de un informe," "El Karuguá," "Ajuste de cuentos," "La rebelión," "Hogar," "Niño-Azoté," "La gran solución," "La excavación."

El pollito de fuego. Buenos Aires: Ediciones de la Flor, 1974.

El ruiseñor de la aurora, y otros poemas. Asunción: Imprenta Nacional, 1942.

Son of Man. Translated by Rachel Caffyn. London: V. Gollancz, 1965. Translation of *Hijo de hombre;* numerous translations into other languages exist.

El trueno entre las hojas; cuentos. Buenos Aires: Losada, 1953. Contents: "Carpincheros," "El viejo Señor Obispo," "El ojo de la muerte," "Mano cruel," "Audiencia privada," "La excavación," Cigarrillos 'Máuser,' "Regreso," "Galopa en dos tiempos," "El Karuguá," "Pirulí," "Esos rostros oscuros," "La rogativa," "La gran solución," "El prisionero," "La tumba viva," "El trueno entre las hojas."

Yo el Supremo. Buenos Aires: Siglo XXI Argentina, 1974.

SECONDARY SOURCES

AGOSTI, HECTOR P. "La problemática de Roa Bastos." In his *La milicia literaria,* pp. 133–37. Buenos Aires: Ediciones Sílaba, 1969. An excellent review by a well-known Marxist critic; stresses the denunciatory aspects of *Hijo de hombre.*

AINSA AMIGUES, FERNANDO. "Un realismo de la imaginación." *Mundo nuevo,* no. 11 (1967), 78–80. An overview of Roa's short stories since *El trueno;* stressed is the "reality of that which we cannot see," a mythic realism that goes beyond documentary socialist realism.

ALDANA, ADELFO LEÓN. *La cuentística de Augusto Roa Bastos.* Montevideo: Ediciones Geminis, 1975. A detailed study of thematic categories and technical-rhetorical procedures in Roa's short stories. An excellent contribution.

――――. "Lo universal en la cuentística de Augusto Roa Bastos." *Explicación de textos literarios* 4, no. 1 (1975), 53–60. Discusses a series of universal/existential thematic constants.

ANDRÉS, ALFREDO. "Ese complejo ser paraguayo." *Sur,* no. 306 (1967), 58–60. Stresses the image of Paraguayans in the stories of *El baldío.*

ANDREU, JEAN L. "*Hijo de hombre* de A. Roa Bastos: fragmentación y unidad." *Revista iberoamericana,* nos. 96–97 (1976), 473–83. Also in *Norte,* unnumbered final issue (1976), 12–25. Essentially covers the same ground as Menton and Foster (1970) on the subject of the multiple narrative voices.

BAREIRO SAGUIER, RUBÉN. "Noción del personaje en *Hijo de hombre.*" *Nueva narrativa hispanoamericana* 4 (1974), 69–74. Also in *Norte,* unnumbered final issue (1976), 26–34. Insists on how, from a semiological point of view, the characters of the novel are not "real" persons, but exponents of literary functions, as are the other, non-human novelistic elements.

――――. "Trayectoria narrativa de Augusto Roa Bastos." *Texto crítico,* no. 4 (1976), 36–46. A rather superficial survey of Roa's fiction.

BARTHELEMY, FRANÇOISE. "Augusto Roa Bastos: de l'auteur unique a l'auteur collectif." *Critique,* nos. 363–364 (1977), 814–830. An excellent general description of the goals of *Yo el Supremo.*

BAZAN, JUAN F. " 'Borrador de un informe.' " In his *La novela latinoamericana,* pp. 141–44. Asunción: Diálogo, 1970. A journalistic note pointing out Roa's merciless dissection of ths contradictions of Paraguayan reality in one of his stories.

BECACECE, HUGO. "*Moriencia,* de Augusto Roa Bastos." *Sur,* no. 320 (1969),

95–98. General characterization of the comprehensive collection of recent stories.

BENEDETTI, MARIO. "El recurso del patriarca." *Revista de crítica literaria hispanoamericana* no. 3 (1976), 55–67. Characterization of the novels by Roa and others on Latin American dictators. Particular emphasis is placed on *Yo el Supremo*.

————. "Roa Bastos entre el realismo y la alucinación." In his *Letras del continente mestizo*, pp. 88–92. Montevideo: Arca, 1967. Also in Helmy F. Giacoman, *Homenaje . . .* , pp. 19–24. A general but extremely perceptive "appreciation" by a major fellow fiction writer.

CODINA, IVERNA. "Paraguay en unz voz." In her *América en la novela*, pp. 165–70. Buenos Aires: Cruz del Sur, 1964. A series of general comments on Paraguay and on *Hijo de hombre*.

Comentarios sobre Yo el Supremo. Asunción: Ediciones "Club del Libro no. 1," 1975. A series of essays by Beatriz Rodríguez Alcalá de González Oddone, Ramiro Domínguez, Adriano Irala Burgos, and Josefina Plá, on diverse aspects de Roa's novel. Only the essay by Domínguez, " 'Yo el Supremo' de Augusto Roa Bastos," pp. 33–48, aspires toward rigorous academic criticism in its use of semiological concepts to discuss temporal and character levels in the novel.

CRUZ-LUIS, ADOLFO. "Dimensión histórica de *Yo el Supremo*." *Casa de las Américas*, No. 95 (1976), 118–27. Concerns the historical backgrounds of the novel.

ESCUDERO, ALFONSO M. "Fuentes de información sobre: Ernesto Sábato, Juan Rulfo, Augusto Roa Bastos, Carlos Droguett." *Taller de letras*, no. 1 (1971), 110–18. A bibliographical listing primarily valuable for its reference to reviews in newspapers and literary magazines.

FOSTER DAVID WILLIAM. "Augusto Roa Bastos' *I the Supreme:* the Image of a Dictator." *Latin American Literary Review*, no. 7 (1975), 31–35. An earlier version of Chapter 5, section II.

————. "The Figure of Christ Crucified as Narrative Symbol in Roa Bastos' *Hijo de hombre*." *Books Abroad* 37 (1963), 16–20. A discussion of the Christ-like figure of Gaspar Mora; incorporated in part as Chapter 3, section III.

————. "La importancia de *Hijo de hombre* de Roa Bastos en la literatura paraguaya." *Duquesne Hispanic Review* 3 (1964), 95–106. A general introduction to Roa; incorporated in part into Chapter 1.

————. *The Myth of Paraguay in the Fiction of Augusto Roa Bastos*. Chapel Hill: University of North Carolina Press, 1969. (UNCSRLL, #80). A nonmyth-criticism analysis of Roa's "mythopoeic" image of Paraguay in his fiction; parts of this earlier study have been rewritten for inclusion in Chapters 2 and 3.

————. "Una nota sobre el punto de vista narrativo en *Hijo de hombre* de Roa Bastos." *Revista iberoamericana* 36 (1970), 643–50. Also in Helmy F.

Giacoman, *Homenaje* . . . , pp. 155–67. Concerns the dual narrative voice in the novel and the juxtaposition of the voice of the intellectual *manqué* and that of a mythic presence. Incorporated as Chapter 3, section V.

————. *"La pensée sauvage* in Roa Bastos' Recent Fiction." *Chasqui* 4, no. 2 (1975), 29–34. A discussion of the story "Moriencia" in terms of "intellectual" trust vs. collective if distorted memory; included in part in Chapter 4, section II.

GIACOMAN, HELMY F., ed. *Homenaje a Augusto Roa Bastos, variaciones interpretativas en torno a su obra.* Long Island City, N.Y.: Anaya-Las Américas, 1973. A collection of essays that are listed separately in this bibliography.

GIFFORD, DAVID ROBERT. "Myth and Reality in *Hijo de hombre,* a Novel by Roa Bastos." *Dissertation Abstracts International* 36 (1975), 1546A–47A (University of New Mexico). Unable to consult.

GUMUCIO, MARIANO BAPTISTA. "La guerra de la sed en la narrativa de Céspedes y Roa Bastos." *Imagen,* no. 51 (1969), 6–7. On the use of thirst as a narrative symbol.

GURZA, ESPERANZA. "El éxito del fracaso en *El trueno entre las hojas* de Augusto Roa Bastos." In Pacific Northwest Conference on Foreign Languages, *Proceedings* 25, no. 1 (1976), 168–72. Unable to consult.

————. "Gaspar ha muerto. ¡Viva el Cristo!" *La palabra y el hombre,* no. 43 (1967), 499–505. Focuses on the central character of chapter 1 of *Hijo de hombre* and on how he is a figure of man crucified by his fate but yet redeemed and immortalized by his own creative efforts.

HERSZENHORN, JAIME. "Reflexiones sobre la temática de los cuentos de Augusto Roa Bastos." In Helmy F. Giacoman, *Homenaje* . . . , pp. 251–66. Thematic study of Roa's stories; rarely goes beyond superficial commentary within the obvious framework of Roa's "vision of a violent Paraguayan reality."

KLEINBERGS, ANDRIS. "Estudio estructural de *Hijo de hombre* de Roa Bastos." *Atenea,* no. 420 (1968), 155–67. Also in Helmy F. Giacoman, *Homenaje* . . . , pp. 187–201. Despite title this study barely goes beyond a rundown of the superficial elements of the novel, although some attempt is made to describe those elements that function to tie the novel together as a whole.

LECHNER, JAN. "Apuntes para el estudio de la prosa de Roa Bastos." *Norte* 12, no. 2 (1971), 28–34. An attack on Foster's monograph. Lechner denies the presence of any coherent elements of Christian or para-Christian symbology in *Hijo de hombre.*

————. "*Augusto Roa Bastos* [bibliography]." *Norte,* unnumbered final issue (1976), 68–70. A listing of works and criticism, the latter curiously deficient.

LEHNERDT, URTE. "Ensayo de interpretación de *Hijo de hombre* a través de su simbolismo cristiano y social." *Revista iberoamericana* 34 (1968),

67–82. Also in Helmy F. Giacoman, *Homenaje* . . . , pp. 169–85. A discussion of the standard Christian symbolism employed in the novel and of the secular "accommodation" to which Roa submits it.

LORENZ, GÜNTER W. "Augusto Roa Bastos . . . ." In his *Diálogo con América Latina*, pp. 271–310. Barcelona: Editorial Pomaire, 1972. An interview; Roa claims that parts of the text are severely distorted. Originally published in German.

LUCHTING, WOLFGANG A. "Time and Transportation in *Hijo de hombre*." *Norte*, unnumbered final issue (1976), 46–56. Originally in *Research Studies* 41 (1973), 98–106. Deals with the figures of Casiano and Cristóbal Jara in *Hijo de hombre*.

MALDAVSKY, DAVID. "Autocrítica: reportaje a Augusto Roa Bastos." *Los libros*, no. 12 (1970), 11–12. An interview; Roa's critical approach to his own work is discussed, and his dissatisfaction with his own fiction is of interest.

——. "Un enfoque semiótico de la narrativa de Roa Bastos: *Hijo de hombre*." In Helmy F. Giacoman, *Homenaje* . . . , pp. 79–95. An analysis of the novel in terms of the three levels of semiotic analysis (syntactic, semantic, and pragmatic), with the work considered as a "communicated message." The novel is shown to be structurally deficient in some respects.

MARTIN, GERALD. "Roa Bastos: basta ya y abajo la bota. 'Collage' crítico-gutural sobre los intelectuales y el pueblo." *Norte*, unnumbered final issue (1976), 57–67. Quotes from Roa on twelve "strategic" topics.

MENTON, SEYMOUR. "Realismo mágico y dualidad en *Hijo de hombre*." *Revista iberoamericana* 33 (1967), 55–70. Also in Helmy F. Giacoman, *Homenaje* . . . , pp. 203–20. Demonstrates how the novel is constructed in terms of a series of (often antithetical) dualities (For example, Spanish versus Guaraní, indigenism versus universality); this duality provides the aesthetic complexity of the work.

MILIANI, DOMINGO. "El dictador: objeto narrativo en *Yo el Supremo*." *Revista de crítica literaria latinoamericana*, no. 4 (1976), 103–19. A discussion of the projection of the dictator, in both sociological and literary terms, in Roa's novel.

MIRET, ENIC. "En torno a *Hijo de hombre*." *Norte*, unnumbered final issue (1976), 35–45. Perfunctory notes on the complex structure of the novel.

MONTERO, JANINA. "Realidad y ficción en *Hijo de hombre*." *Revista iberoamericana*, no. 95 (1976), 267–74. Studies the alternating chapters of the novel on the basis of a dialectical opposition "hero/antihero." Does not go much beyond Foster (1970).

PASSAFARI DE GUTIÉRREZ, CLARA. "La condición humana en la narrativa de Roa Bastos." *Universidad* [Santa Fe], no. 46 (1960), 137–61. Also in Helmy F. Giacoman, *Homenaje* . . . , pp. 25–45. *Hijo* . . . deals not just with the Paraguayan circumstance, but with a universal condition of mankind; a valuable alternative to "localist" interpretations.

PICCINI, MABEL. "El trueno entre las hojas y el humanismo revolucionario."
Cuadernos del Instituto de Literatura Argentina e Iberoamericana, no. 1
(1965), 6–15. Also in Helmy F. Giacoman, *Homenaje . . .* , pp. 237–49.
A general thematic survey, with emphasis on the stories' "humanistic
commitment to a collective tragedy."

PUEBLA, MANUEL DE LA. "El estilo de la narrativa de Augusto Roa Bastos."
In Helmy F. Giacoman, *Homenaje . . .* , pp. 47–62. Stresses how, even
in his novels, Roa's principal narrative techniques are those of the short
story; other comments are quite superficial.

ROBLES, HUMBERTO E. "El círculo y la cruz en *Hijo de hombre*." *Nueva
narrativa hispanoamericana* 4 (1974), 193–219. Study of the symbolic
function in the novel of the circle (the cyclical pattern of life) and the
cross (the redemption of manking); one of the only truly mythic
interpretations of the novel.

RODRÍGUEZ ALCALÁ, HUGO. "Augusto Roa Bastos y *El trueno entre las hojas*."
Revista iberoamericana, no. 39 (1955), 19–45. Also in his *Korn, Romero,
Güiraldes, Unamuno, Ortega, literatura paraguaya y otros ensayos*
(Mexico City: Studium, 1958), pp. 171–98. The only extensive review of
Roa's first book of stories; what is stressed is the unifying thread of
violence and the synthetic vision of Paraguay.

———. "Un experimento borgiano: 'La excavación.' " *La palabra y el
hombre*, no. 41 (1967), 5–17. Also as "Jorge Luis Borges en 'La
excavación', de Augusto Roa Bastos," in *El cuento hispanoamericano
ante la crítica*, ed. Enrique Pupo-Walker (Madrid: Editorial Castalia,
1973), pp. 179–94; and in Helmy F. Giacoman, *Homenaje . . .* , pp.
221–35. The influence of Borges's stories on Roa's text, involving both
verbal style and "ideas" concerning atemporal parallelism of men and
events; unconvincing.

———. "Un experimento fallido: 'El pájaro mosca.' " *Humanitas* [Monter-
rey], no. 10 (1969), 387–400. Also in his *Narrativa hispanoamericana
. . .* (Madrid: Editorial Gredos, 1973), pp. 63–81. Discusses one of Roa's
few stories not based on popular elements and problems: intellectual
rivalry is involved and the story is shown to be unsatisfactory in narrative
development.

———. "*Hijo de hombre* de Roa Bastos y la intrahistoria del Paraguay."
Cuadernos americanos, no. 121 (1963), 221–34. Also in Helmy F.
Giacoman, *Homenaje . . .* , pp. 63–78. Roa's novel manifests a major
unifying coherency, a trajectory of Paraguayan history, not documentary
but rather collectively unconscious.

———. "El sentido universalista del *Hijo de hombre* de Roa Bastos o la
intrahistoria del Paraguay." In his *Sugestión e ilusión: ensayos de
estilística e ideas*, pp. 75–97. Xapala: Universidad Veracruzana, Facul-
tad de Filosofía y Letras, 1967. A different version of preceding entry.

———. "Verdad oficial y verdad verdadera: 'Borrador de un informe' de
Augusto Roa Bastos." *Cuadernos americanos*, no. 156 (1968), 251–67.

Selected Bibliography

Selected Bibliography

Selected Bibliography 131

Also in his *Narrativa hispanoamericana . . . (* Madrid: Editorial Gredos, 1973), pp. 39–62. Also in Helmy F. Giacoman, *Homenaje . . .* , pp. 277–94; and as "Official Truth and 'True' Truth: Augusto Roa Bastos' 'Borrador de un informe,' " *Studies in Short Fiction* 8 (1971), 141–54. Focus is on the story as a particularly representative example of Roa's complex narrative art, which involves a "self-conscious" interest in technical difficulties.

RODRÍGUEZ RICHART, J. " 'Mano cruel,' narración picaresca de Roa Bastos." *Boletín de la Biblioteca Menéndez Pelayo* 45 (1969), 239–54. A rather tedious and pointless description of one of Roa's minor stories.

RUIZ, MARIO E. "La introspección auto-crítica en 'Contar un cuento.' " In Helmy F. Giacoman, *Homenaje . . .* , pp. 267–76. An explication of the story, stressing its exemplariness in terms of the "author-reader complicity" emphasized by contemporary Latin American fiction.

Seminario sobre Yo el Supremo de Augusto Roa Bastos. Poitiers: Centre de Recherches Latino-Américaines de l'Université de Poitiers, 1976. Collection of critical essays presented at a symposium held in April, 1976, at the university.

SOMMERS, JOSEPH. "Un juicio sobre *Hijo de hombre.*" *Alcor,* no. 33 (1964), 4a. A "general identification" of the novel.

TREVISÁN, LILÍ OLGA. "Literatura de una tierra joyosa. Su novelística: Augusto Roa Bastos." *Revista de literaturas modernas,* no. 6 (1967), 79–107. After a survey of historical and cultural backgrounds of Paraguay, there is a brief presentation of important recent writers and a survey of Roa's literary production.

VALDÉS, ADRIANA, and RODRÍGUEZ, IGNACIO. "*Hijo de hombre:* el mito como fuerza social." *Taller de letras,* no. 1 (1971), 75–95. Also in Helmy F. Giacoman, *Homenaje . . .* , pp. 97–154. The novel is studied as a fictional myth that creates a particular vision of the Paraguayan; that myth may be seen as a "social force" in its message to readers.

Index

DATE DUE

RETURNED